SCIENCE, INDUSTRY

AND

SOCIAL POLICY

"AN ISLAND"

An industrial scene by L. S. Lowry: in the collection of the
City Art Gallery, Manchester.

The preference of the English well-to-do classes for country
life is probably one of the important reasons why the industrial
towns and the industrial environment developed even more offensively in Britain than abroad. Much of industry's profit was
transferred to areas far from where it was made. But sometimes,
as in Lowry's scene, industry caught up with the country houses
and the occupants departed (ch. IV).

SCIENCE, INDUSTRY
AND
SOCIAL POLICY

KENNETH DENBIGH

OLIVER & BOYD

EDINBURGH AND LONDON

OLIVER AND BOYD LTD.

Tweeddale Court
Edinburgh

39a Welbeck Street
London w.1.

First published   1963

Printed in Great Britain by The Central Press (Aberdeen) Ltd.

PREFACE

This essay, which is a brief social criticism of applied science and industry, originated from an Inaugural Lecture at Edinburgh. I am much indebted to Professor Youngson of that University for useful comments on an early version of Chapter II, and to my wife and others who have also been very helpful.

K. G. D.

Edinburgh & London
   1958-1962

CONTENTS

CHAPTER I

INDUSTRIAL SOCIETY MOVING INTO
A NEW PHASE

WHAT new forms of social progress can we achieve in our modern industrial societies—forms different in kind from those hitherto regarded as important? I believe this question is present in many people's thoughts, not least among scientists and engineers. There is a widespread feeling that our current philosophy of social progress has become fixed and stereotyped, that our concepts of economic advance and the standard of living are far too limited and that we must go beyond them if we are to build for our civilization a satisfying future.

Much of what follows is based on the view that in Western countries a certain psychological phase of industrialism is coming to an end. Industrialism, I suggest, is now approaching the completion of its early immature period and is moving towards a second phase which will entail a change of emphasis and a redefining of objectives. Yet this phase has not yet properly begun* and the whole character of industrialism is still essentially primitive—that is when the matter is thought of in regard to objectives rather than methods and when the word primitive is used, not in a derogatory sense, but rather as referring to the first period of an era.

This era is usually regarded as having begun in Britain about 1780 and the primitive phase has been the creating of the modern industrial system accompanied by a great concentration of interest on economics and techniques. Obviously

---

* It is often said that a Second Industrial Revolution is now taking place but this refers to the technical methods of industry and not to its purposes.

enough this process will go a long way further; even in the advanced economies there is still a good deal of poverty and poor housing and for this reason alone further expansion of these economies is greatly to be desired. Also there are recurrent economic crises due to countries wanting to consume more than they are willing or able to produce. Yet by and large, if the matter is thought of in relation to the Western world as a whole (which is to say quite apart from the requirements of the underdeveloped areas), the original aims of industrialism are being steadily achieved. Production remains an important " problem ", and especially from the standpoint of competition, but it is no longer a problem in the sense of something unsolved, something which brings out the kind of intellectual and emotional powers which it did earlier. " The rich Western countries," writes Gunnar Myrdal,[1] " have by now reached the stage where, in each of them taken individually, further economic progress has become almost automatic."

It would seem that Britain has gone further than other countries in completing this early stage of industrialization— or at least in the psychological sense which is here being discussed. The factory system has been with us a relatively long time and the zest and enthusiasm and the other attitudes of mind which gave force to the 19th century drive for production, no longer have their 19th century intensity. I believe it is true to say that economic motivation has now become less strong in Britain—and this at all levels of society—than in other countries whose " industrial revolutions " occurred later. We are now a nation of shopkeepers much less than many of our neighbours.

If the original ethos of industrialism is losing its vitality in Britain, a new one is badly wanted. The existing signs of lassitude may have several causes, but one of them is that the attainment of many of the earlier objectives has left us in a kind of vacuum; the industrial order is now more in need of a new idea of itself in Britain than it is almost anywhere else.

In brief I am suggesting that economic revival itself may not occur except as the consequence of new objectives at a level deeper than the economic; if we can find the right spirit and the guiding idea of how we wish to progress, the economic side of things may be expected to look after itself.

However, this is not a purely British question and this essay was not written with only the British future of industrialism in mind. In much of the Western world there is a certain scepticism about what passes as progress and also the feeling that, as C. P. Snow puts it, " we are beginning to shrug off our sense of the future . . . we haven't any model of the future before us."[2]

A One-Sided Development

If imagination has not yet prepared itself for the next phase, no doubt one of the reasons is that a very uneven development has been taking place during the past two hundred years and men's thoughts have become fixed in certain channels. Technological change has rushed over the West, as it is now rushing over other parts of the world; trade and industry have expanded immensely and economic considerations have taken on an almost pre-emptive character—far more so than during earlier periods when living conditions were poor by modern standards and when a preoccupation with economic affairs might therefore have seemed more necessary. Modern societies have been fascinated and overcome by their new resources and have not yet found a clear enough vision how to reconcile industrialism with all else that is needed to make a civilization which is humanly satisfying. The immense gains in living standards have been achieved at a certain cost. An earlier European conception of civilization was based on the balancing of various interests—commercial, aesthetic, communal—and this helped to maintain a sense of quality and style and also a sense of mutual obligation and service. But this conception has been allowed to diminish in influence and the commercial side of affairs has become overwhelming.

Our aim, I believe, should be to build up a balanced culture in modern terms—and this must mean the fostering of interests and values complementary to the commercial and economic interests which the past two centuries have been mainly concerned with.

Obviously enough we shall want economic activity to be maintained and increased, and one important reason, quite apart from our continuing requirement for private goods, is the need for the much increased flow of funds into the public sector which Galbraith and others have called for. An even more important reason is the financial assistance so urgently required by the underdeveloped areas. Beyond that there is the psychological necessity to compete, to keep up with the Jones in a national sense, and this cannot be shrugged off.

All this may be agreed. Yet the burden of what I have to say is that if we are to move into a more advanced stage of industrial civilization, the earlier view of what industrialism is about—the view that it is concerned almost entirely with the economic side of things—will prove far too restricted.

And in fact many of the present problems of Western societies are very far from being economic in character. Associated with industrialism as we know it there is a general atmosphere of makeshift and unstable values; large numbers of people among the industrial population have an almost complete lack of interest in what they do; work itself provides no real centre or meaning to their lives; and education has not yet done enough, by way of the awakening of personal interests, to help them find satisfaction or fulfilment outside the working hours.

In brief, it is my contention that the reorientation of the industrial order needs to be achieved in a social much more than in a purely economic sense. If our society is lacking in purpose we have the need to formulate new objectives—

objectives we can believe in and be willing to work for. No doubt this will require the overhaul of many of our fundamental assumptions and this may be a daunting business (innovation of a conceptual kind being about the most difficult kind of innovation to achieve). Yet this should now be one of politics' most important tasks. The recovery of an active spirit of reform, leading to a transformation of our society wherever it is needed (and the energies which such a transformation would release), is surely the means by which the West can regain its strength.

Industrialism as a Continuing Process

This essay is thus conceived as a commentary on the social aspects of applied science and industry. Among the factors to be considered are the effects of industrialism on the quality of the urban environment; on the amount of interest and satisfaction obtainable from the working day; on the retention of a firm sense of personal direction by men and women living under industrial conditions. In these and other respects—and in spite of vastly improved living standards— our modern society is perhaps backward as compared to Europe of the 12th-16th centuries.

Since that time the most significant social change has been the emergence of large scale industry—and this is a process which will surely be at least equal in its effects to those earlier transformations of man's economy, the Agricultural and Urban Revolutions (as they were called by Gordon Childe). These were likewise the causes of drastic disturbances to the existing states of society and during their early stages may have appeared as being chaotic and haphazard, as creating more problems than they solved. Yet the terminal effects of the development of agriculture, and later of city life, were great refinements in living—the advancement of the arts and sciences, and of man's sensibility and knowledge.

This very comparison suggests that industrialism is likely to be a continuing process and that at present it may still be in a precursory form. The Agricultural and Urban Revolutions were very far from being revolutions in the sense of changes which almost suddenly attained their ends. Their social consequences occurred continuously over millenia and, with these analogies in mind, it seems likely that the assimilation of modern industry may prove almost equally slow.

And this assimilation, as it takes place, will not necessarily be on the same lines in all countries. The influence of different traditions, varying from one part of the world to another, may be expected to cause important regional differences in the manner and spirit in which industrialism evolves.

Related to this is the important question of the American way of living. Should the smaller or less well endowed industrial countries, Britain included, allow themselves to move very far in the direction of the American style of economy? Or indeed could they hope to keep up with it, even if they wished? In England it is becoming obvious that some features of American living—low density housing areas and the aim of two or three cars to the family—are not compatible with the smallness of the land. Apart from that there is the question of natural resources. The United States is prodigal in its consumption and uses up a quite disproportionate amount of the world's total timber and minerals. It may be that Russia, which is also a sparsely populated country of immense resources, will develop a similar society to the American—similar in consumption if not in politics.

Other countries may need to take a different path. Something that Britain and Western Europe could do is to develop a style of industrial society different from that of the U.S.— and different also from that of Russia—something well adapted to their own situation and which might be further modified by the countries of Asia. Both in Western Europe and in Southern Asia the populations are large in relation to the quantities of natural resources. Though they differ immensely in other respects, what both areas may need are forms of industrial society making interest and well-being for their peoples at levels of consumption which are not too excessive—an emphasis on the quality of life rather than on the quantity of goods.

For these various reasons there is the scope for a more conscious spirit of criticism concerning the forms and assumptions of industrialism and the uses of the economy and of applied science. On a very modest scale, and with no blueprint in mind, I shall try to indicate the main lines along which, as it seems to me, this kind of discussion can be useful. The criticism of what we do at present is the necessary first step towards the formulation of new social policy.

CHAPTER II

THE RISE OF ECONOMICISM

From Obligation to Laissez-Faire

THE Hammonds have written of the 18th and 19th centuries: ". . . the age had turned aside from making a society in order to make a system of production."[1] We may well ask whether our own ideas concerning the purposes of applied science and industry have made much progress since then, and whether we are yet making a society as distinct from an immense output of goods.

The period of early industrialism was preoccupied with building up the source of this output and for this purpose made tacit assumptions concerning priorities which were useful enough in their time—but only in their time. Yet these same assumptions, as Keynes[2] and Galbraith[3] have remarked, have been passed down to us almost unquestioned. Having become part of our inheritance of fixed ideas, they keep us from forming a comprehensive enough view of industry in its modern social context.

To see these matters in perspective it may be useful to go some way back into European history and to retrace the course by which the assumptions of early industrialism gathered their strength. Also these assumptions need to be seen in relation to the social and economic ideas of the Middle Ages and the Renaissance, periods which had their own views on the purposes of the economy distinct in many respects from the doctrines which developed later.

One can begin by recalling how the economic thought of the Middle Ages was conditioned by the circumstances of the time and especially by the first need which was order and security. Still in process of emerging from a state of near chaos, the prevailing emphasis was on protection within the walled cities and on coherence and stability in the social structure. Typical of the restraints on industry and commerce which were the results of these requirements were that the man of business was accepted only on sufferance, whilst, being even more socially disruptive, the taking of interest for money was a crime.[4]

Of course this is not to say that the people of the Middle Ages had no desire for personal gain. Far from it, as is evident from the stringency of some of the precautions drawn up by state and guild. This was a period of active trade and it enjoyed an expanding economy, at least up to the end of the 13th century. But the important point is that the established social theory gave no sanction to the idea of economic activity as an end in itself. What was believed in by society at large (and however far from it the practices of individuals may have deviated) was " commonwealth " far more than increase of private wealth. This was supported by the immense influence of the Church, at the time far more attracted to the idea of a structured society than to the idea of the individual.

Although passion and violence were rife in the Middle Ages, there was also a notable conception of community and mutual obligation. The communal idea shows itself, for example, in the way in which much of the product of the economy was actually used. After the minimal personal requirements of food, clothing and so forth had been met, much of the remainder went towards consolidating the community as a whole. The amount so used was high relative to modern custom, a conspicuous example being the immense expenditure on the building of churches and cathedrals.*

* Jean Gimpel[5] estimates that the construction of churches and cathedrals involved, in France alone between 1050 and 1350, the quarrying of a volume of stone greater than was used in Ancient Egypt during the whole of its history.

2

Although this form of expenditure is commonly regarded as having been an expression solely of the religious spirit is was probably just as much an expression of the communal outlook and of civic pride. Construction had virtually ceased by the 14th and 15th centuries, which was long before there was any great falling off in religious fervour. The cathedrals, built large enough to hold all members of the community under one roof, were the centres of the corporate life of the cities; they acted as public halls, as places where treasure and deeds could be stored and business transacted, as well as places of worship.

The same communal idea, and especially in regard to obligation, may be seen in the structure of the productive system itself. The aim of the guilds, before they decayed, was to draw their members together as a closely knit unit, preventing one member from advancing himself at the expense of another and safeguarding their reputation by the enforcement of adequate standards. The system was thus conservative and protective; the guild members were protected not only from competition from without but also from each other; advertisement was forbidden[6] and it was not unknown for inventions to be suppressed if deemed desirable in the interests of the town or of fellow members of the guild.[7]

Although this idea of an ordered social structure determined how much of the product of the economy was created and used during the earlier part of the Middle Ages, this was no longer so during the later part when individualism had become a much stronger force. Typical of the change was the outlook of men such as Brunelleschi and Leonardo. Brunelleschi, for example, was in revolt against the careful anonymity which the guilds had imposed on the work of the architect and he was determined that the great dome should be known by his name, and by his name only. It may be recalled how he became involved in a long drawn out struggle with the masons—a struggle in which the guild masters managed to have him put in prison for non-payment of his membership fees, and that at a time when he was already famous and the dome was rising high above Florence.[8]

The expression of the acquisitive instincts, as well as this spirit of individualism, also became much more socially allowable. The effect of the Renaissance, and of the mounting strength of capitalism, was to give these instincts much greater freedom. Thus already by the end of the 15th century Leonardo revealed himself quite openly: " Early to-morrow, Jan. 2, 1496, I shall make the leather belt and proceed to a trial . . . one hundred times in each hour 400 needles will be finished, making 40,000 in an hour and 480,000 in twelve hours. Suppose we say 4,000 thousands (implying 10 machines) which at 5 solidi per thousand gives 20,000 solidi : 1000 lira per working day, and if one works 20 days in the month 60,000 ducats the year."

The decline of the Middle Ages thus coincides with the emergence of a new attitude towards industry, an attitude which was to develop its strength over several centuries and was based on the use of capital and machines, and the expectation of profit. At a time when security had already been achieved, the emphasis turned to the private accumulation of wealth.

Already within the guilds, by the 13th and 14th centuries, the more powerful of the master craftsmen had begun to assert themselves and had built up hereditary businesses which used the paid services of the lesser craftsmen as employees and farmed out to them the means of production.* Also there developed an increasing specialization of function whereby the craftsmen no longer sold their products direct to the consumers, but instead sold to the merchants who in turn sold to the retailers. And at a yet higher level in the

---

* The scope for capitalism was especially great in the textile, mining and metal industries and it has been claimed that there were several factories employing workers in considerable numbers before the close of the Middle Ages.

new system, supplying credit equally to merchants and princes, and to entrepreneurs of all kinds, were the great families of bankers. Such were the Medici and Strozzi of Florence, and the Fuggers of Augsburg. The rise of banking from its beginnings in the commercial cities of Italy[9] is no doubt one of the decisive factors at the origin of modern industry.

These changes, taking place from the 14th century onwards, and affecting forms of consumption as well as of production, were later strongly reinforced, in Protestant countries at least, by the decline in the wealth and power of the Church. For whereas the Church, from its entrenched position as a landlord, had formerly been an important user of technical resources, this was no longer the case after the Reformation. Hence there occurred a major shift in the use of the product of the economy—from the communal and religious to the private and secular. And simultaneously one of the effects of the doctrines of the reformed Churches was to fortify the notions of the individual conscience, of individual responsibility—and thus gradually, of enterprise, opportunity ... and profit!

The Renaissance and Reformation periods were therefore, from an economic viewpoint, the assertion of the value of money over the value of land, and, from a sociological viewpoint, the assertion of the idea of the individual over the idea of the community.

One important result was the impetus given to art—but art which was mainly for private use. The stonemasons and architects, the goldsmiths and the weavers of silk, were now working for a different kind of employer and, in place of the cathedrals, there rose up in great commercial centres like Florence and Bruges the marvellous houses of the bankers and merchants. Great families such as the Medici were able to use their liquid assets for the purposes of private art to an extent undreamed of by the feudal landlords of the Middle

Ages. The Renaissance and its aftermath were periods when the brightest spirits had an immense zest for artistic creation and also for technology: it was a technico-artistic culture where the useful and the fine arts had not yet separated, but whose greatest benefits were the privilege of only a very small number.

This new exclusiveness in the use of the product of the economy was perhaps less marked in England than in most of the continental countries. England, it seems, was already moving, by the end of the 16th century, towards the production of relatively cheap commodities, based on cast iron.[10] But on the continent it was taken for granted that one of the main purposes of technology was the creation of works of art for the few, and it was this, allied very often to a love of the stupendous,[11] which there set the tone of technology from the Renaissance until comparatively modern times.

The Ascendance of the Profit Motive

In Britain the far-reaching changes which led up to the modern system of production were those of the late 18th and early 19th centuries—the period which has come to be known, for better or for worse, as the industrial revolution. It was the time of the great inventions and the rapid development of coal and steam; of the great increase in the productive power of capital; of the more widespread distribution of the product of the economy; and further (and perhaps the most important as an intellectual legacy) of the writings of the " classical economists "—Adam Smith, Bentham and later Ricardo and others—men who have decisively influenced the whole outlook of modern times.

It would surely be quite unjust to regard these authors as having been responsible for everything that was subsequently done in the name of *laissez-faire*; the age read into them what it wanted to read and used their authority to justify desires which had long existed.[12] Clearly there was nothing

new in commerce wanting greater liberty and less control.
Nor was there anything new in the expression of acquisitive-
ness. For a long time commerce had been a kind of dominant
passion and with it an intense interest in goods and property.

What was essentially new in the late 18th and early 19th
centuries was something rather different. It was the belief
that the operations of commerce *should* be free; that complete
freedom was in the interests of the nation as well as of the
individual; that any form of social restraint was not only
harmful to commerce but harmful to society as a whole. And
thus the profit motive rose to a position of great ascendance.
And with this went the outlook—the residue of which is still
to be overcome—that the only obligation of industry is
economic, that it has no functions or responsibilities to society
other than to provide profit, goods and wages.

Associated with these changes and affecting their character
were several important factors: the declining industrial
interest and influence of members of the aristocracy and the
rise to industrial leadership of the middle classes; the
influence of non-conformism and the somewhat contrary influence, in the 19th century, of the Romantic movement; and
finally, in more recent times, the increasing sense of social
conscience.

Of the upper classes' earlier interest in technology and
industry there is ample evidence: the custom in Elizabethan
England for the younger sons of the gentry to become apprentices in manufacturing establishments; the original aim of
the Royal Society of stimulating improvements in the useful
arts; the work of the Earls of Bedford in draining the Fens
and the agricultural advances of Lord Townshend and Coke
of Norfolk. Interest in technology and industry from such
quarters may have reached its peak in the 18th century. But
already by this time new forces and new men were coming
to the fore and it was no longer the aristocratic families,
whose fortunes had been founded on commerce at an earlier

period, who provided the main impulse towards technical or commercial innovation. Many of the leading figures— men such as Arkwright, Boulton and Watt—came from a very different level of society.* Industry was the stepping stone for advancement and was instrumental in the creation of a powerful and prosperous middle class.

One of the effects of the diminished aristocratic interest in the " useful arts " was a change in their social status and a more restricted concept of their purpose. The place of technology as a cultured interest was taken over by pure science—and its " purity " was a comparatively new idea unknown to the founders of the Royal Society. As the result the useful arts became further separated from the fine arts[13] and were regarded to an increasing extent as being solely economic in purpose. What the new business leaders wanted from technology was the making of money; with this they achieved the greatness of Britain and the squalor of the slag heaps.

Yet another important factor in shaping the character of industrialism was the continuing influence of Calvinism and Puritanism. Combined with an emphasis on practical ethics and strenuous work there was a repudiation of the pleasure of art. " You may labour to be *Rich for God,* though not for the *flesh* and sin."[14] And therefore if a man must work hard, but is abjured from the enjoyment of luxury, he has a strong incentive to plough back his profit into his business. At least one cause of the rapid industrial expansion of England and Scotland, and also the outlook of aesthetic indifference, must surely be attributed to the influence of Calvinism and later of non-conformism.[15]

---

* According to Mantoux (*La Revolution Industrielle au XVIIIe siècle,* Paris 1906) the great majority of the new industrialists were of country origin and were descended from farmers or small proprietors. Actually very few of the well-known inventors became leaders of business; the latter had to have the ability to organize and this did not often go with inventiveness. (See also Pevsner, *Pioneers of the Modern Movement,* Ch. II, Faber & Faber, 1936.)

But that is not all; this influence tended towards an interest in applied science, as well towards a policy of reinvestment.[16] Excluded from the universities during the 18th century, the non-conformists founded their own teaching academies and gave them a strong scientific leaning. Better adapted to the requirements of the time than Oxford and Cambridge, where science was in a state of decay, these academies were at the forefront of the technological movement and provided the education of many of the leading industrialists. The Darbys of Coalbrookdale, and many simliar figures, it will be recalled, were Quakers. One of the results was that applied science became associated with an attitude of piety and hard work. Yet to the Quakers and other non-conformists there was nothing inconsistent with their religious outlook in the founding of great family fortunes, provided it was done in a spirit of frugality and the service of God.

In quite a different direction lay the influence of the type of Romantic movement which developed in restricted circles in Britain towards the end of the 18th and during the 19th centuries. Here the interest was more in nature than in man's works; in feeling more than in rationality; in ideals more than in utility. One of the consequences among those who were influenced was a desire to hold themselves apart from the factory system. In contrast to many of the artists of the early 18th century who had portrayed the rising industry of the time with great zest and enthusiasm, an important group of painters of the Romantic movement began to put forward images of industry as scenes of horror.[17] From the side of the writers also, Southey, Ruskin and many others were starting to make vigorous protest against almost everything that was being done by industry in the name of progress.

Ruskin, it will be remembered, was vigorously outspoken when he addressed the industrialists of Bradford and put forward a strong criticism of the capitalist system: it had reduced the majority of mankind to the status of available labour and, far from providing the kind of work in which men could fulfil and create themselves (one of the true purposes of the social order), what it had actually provided was labour which was so much drudgery, if not actually degrading.[18]

During the 19th century there had thus opened up a deep division in the upper reaches in Britain: on the one side were the industrialists riding on a triumphant wave (and they included some such as Brunel who were men of vision); on the other were many of the outstanding writers—men such as Ruskin and Morris who were sensitive to what was wrong with industrialism but whose protest was not entirely effective due to their failure to develop an alternative economic theory with sufficient rigour.

Also, of course, there were the members of the peerage; many had detached themselves from industrialism in the spirit whilst continuing to live on their mining and industrial investments. Towards this aristocratic layer many of the intellectuals having similar feelings tended to gravitate and there was thus formed the characteristic anti-industrialism of upper-class and literary society—a phenomenon which seems to have been by no means confined to Britain.[19]

That so many of the philosophers, poets and artists had thus parted company from the industrialists and engineers was surely to the detriment of a far more imaginative and more liberal use of the new resources. Their influence was absent where it was needed and the effect of their turning away was to confirm an anti-intellectual and anti-aesthetic tendency on the industrial side. Confined to the world of business, the industrial leaders conceived the aims of technology in the narrowest of economic terms; as the making of profit and the building up of the new industrial families, together with their shareholders, lawyers and accountants.

Yet the industrial order had become not only anti-intellectual and anti-aesthetic but also, in a deeper sense, anti-social —and had been for a long time. The idea of the solidarity and interdependence of the classes, so marked a feature of the social theory of the Middle Ages, had been gradually eroded and replaced by an entirely different outlook. Its meaning may be seen clearly enough in the structure of company law. For whereas in medieval social theory, lord and vassal and serf were under *mutual* obligation (the weaker giving service to the stronger, and the stronger giving protection to the weaker) this reciprocal relationship had no counterpart in the joint-stock companies. In the event of business failure the debenture holders and shareholders took what was left and these latter, called the " owners " of the company, were not regarded as having any responsibility to provide for the discharged workers. In the circumstances of this kind of system (much of which still exists) it is not surprising that Andrew Ure could write in 1835 that one of the great virtues of technology was that it was the answer to the insubordination of labour: " . . . when capital enlists science in her service, the refractory hand of labour will always be taught docility."[20]

Shall we not see some of the characteristics of the period as a consequence of the ideas of economics having been applied too freely to ordinary life? Theories are abstractions and it has been one of the failings of the industrial age that it has taken economic theory in a very literal sense, or has regarded the theory as if it were applicable to the social life in its entirety.

The Emergence of Welfare

During the present century society has come to regard the purposes of industry and technology in a rather different light; it has been seen that industry, as well as being concerned with output, has certain responsibilities to its workers and especially concerning continuity of employment; also it has been found a social and economic necessity that the product of industry should be distributed fairly evenly over the whole population, employers and workers in like manner. From the side of the employers Henry Ford developed a clear idea of the advantages to an expanding economy of increasing the purchasing power of the employees: ". . . I want to distribute the maximum of wage—that is, the maximum of buying power."[21] From the side of the workers the socialist and trade union movements took action to rectify the conditions of the previous century and to obtain for the employee better conditions of work and a larger share of his output.

Industry and technology are thus no longer seen as being the servants of a particular social class, but rather as being the means towards a general state of well-being. Applied science now serves distinctively social aims and the governments of the major countries have to concern themselves continually with technical advance. When one thinks of the vast amount of work being done by government laboratories and hospitals, by universities and colleges, and by international agencies, in fields such as the peaceful use of nuclear energy, smoke abatement, the efficient use of fuel, public health and medicine, agriculture and fisheries, forestry and the conservation of natural resources, one begins to form a concept of technology as a form of public service which is in marked contrast to the idea which was held in the 19th century.

Of course it is still the case that the main aim of the economic system is the supply of private rather than of public goods.[22] Yet it would be no more than a half-truth to suppose that it is only a selfish materialism which determines the economy. The worldwide movement towards industrialism is something much more than that and has an ethical as well as a materialistic character. The moral argument for the machine is everywhere the same: it is the belief that ever increasing sections of the world's population should have the fulness of life formerly available only to the few; this means not only improved living conditions but also better opportunities for each individual to fulfil himself and the necessary provision of more extensive education.[23]

Economicism and Beyond

Despite all these advances the general attitude towards industry remains as equivocal and complex as it has been for over a century. One significant sign of this, to be seen not least among scientists and industrialists, is the preference in private life for whatever is old and pre-industrial: for antique furniture, for old houses, for well-settled country towns or villages. At a much deeper level there is undoubtedly a strong sense of disquiet about industrialism as a whole. What has been said with varying emphasis by a long line of imaginative writers—Southey, Ruskin, Dickens, Morris, D. H. Lawrence and others up to the present day—finds a certain echo in almost everyone. There is in fact a widespread ambivalence of outlook; one which is appreciative of the good things of industry and yet regards industry as destructive.

This divided state of mind would appear as one of the signs that industrialism has not yet been properly assimilated and taken in; it is still the hard stone against which society hurts itself. Towards agriculture, that other means of production, we have no corresponding sense of uncertainty; it has been in existence for so much longer and has become woven into the whole social fabric; we regard it as a way of life, as well as a source of food. Until industry has become similarly advanced in a social sense the conflicting attitudes to it will continue: an active rejection as in Lawrence; an excessive enthusiasm as with the early Futurists; more usually a certain holding back, an incomplete acceptance.

When it is recalled that the factory system is still only a few generations old, the fact that our society has not yet adapted itself successfully to the new conditions is not surprising. Some of the signs of what I have called the still primitive character of industrialism are the spendthrift use of natural resources, the chaotic and haphazard character of the industrial environment, and the general sense of temporariness and instability. Almost wherever industry exists one is in the presence of something uncouth and unformed.

A further indication that industrialism has not yet properly come of age is the kind of idea we have of it. The earlier view that its main purpose is private gain has been happily almost superseded and has been replaced by an idea of industry as serving society as a whole. Yet we still think of this service as being economic *and nothing more.* As compared to agriculture, industry is still at the stage where it is thought of as being only so much output and money; that is to say, we tend to think of the industrial system almost entirely in economic, hardly at all in completely social terms.

Without prejudice to the importance of economics as a science, the view that economic factors are the only significant ones in society may be called *economicism.** The great achievement of economics has been to bring into *one part* of the social life a certain scientific precision. However there have been influences which have caused this part to be seen highly magnified and as if it were the whole. What I mean by economicism is the attitude which accepts that it is the whole.

To make this point at a little greater length, it may be said that one of the major difficulties in forming a conception of social well-being as having more than an economic aspect arises from the desire for measurability. In a scientific world where number is so important it is the things which are most easily measured which are most completely believed in, whereas many of those which are not measurable have come

---

* Cf. *Scientism* which has an analogous meaning.

to seem almost unreal.* With regard to social well-being, as
Pigou has remarked, only the economic part can be expressed
quantitatively: " The one obvious instrument of measure-
ment available in social life is money."[24] Thus the monetary
measure of things comes to seem all-important.†

A well-known example of where this sort of calculus fails
is its inability to include in its scope those kinds of work
and service which are outside the market system. In the
meaning of economics work which is not paid for (because
this means it is not measurable) cannot be counted as productive work. This applies, for example, to what the wife does
for her home, what the parents do for their children, what the
city councillor does for his city, and generally to all forms of
voluntary duty. When economic theory cannot include these
as being an important part of what happens in society, it is
not surprising that, when economicism becomes the dominant
mode of thought, great harm is done to the sense of mutual
obligation and service.

Of course in certain contexts the economic part of social
well-being may well be an adequate measure of the whole, or
an economic advance may be an overall advance. Yet there
are important contrary instances where steps which are taken

* Another important example occurs in education where the important non-
examinable element in good education tends to get overlooked. The merit of
schools comes to be judged in terms of the number of their Oxbridge
scholarships and the merit of students by their positions in the examination
lists.

† It is not meant to suggest that economics should not seek to be quantitative. Far from it; the harmful effects of what I have called economicism
arise mainly from the fact that conventional costing procedures cover only
a part of the total social situation. The further extension of quantitative
methods (e.g. by attempting to give costing a wider scope) is a useful line
of advance and an interesting example of what can be done has been
indicated in two articles by C. D. Foster in The Times (11 and 12 Dec.,
1962—also in more detail in a paper submitted by C. D. Foster and M. E.
Beesley to The Royal Statistical Society). Here the value of constructing
the Victoria Underground is discussed by the methods of social benefit cost
analysis; in addition to ordinary profit costing this includes putting a
monetary value to such factors as gain in traveller's comfort, saving of
people's time, and so on. Much might be hoped for if this kind of analysis
could be extended to other aspects of modern industrialism.

to assist the economy may otherwise be harmful.* And again some of the consequences of industrialism, to be discussed more fully later, have been seriously anti-social.

In writing as I have done it may seem that I am taking up an anti-business standpoint, but that is far from my intention. The man who creates a new and flourishing business may be giving work to people who previously had none, or he may be helping them to support themselves far more adequately than before. Commercial activity—whether one's own or one's country's—is also a matter of natural and absorbing interest. My concern is only to suggest that, since the 18th century, a certain oversimplified view of society has become widespread. Economic criteria have come to be accepted as if they were the only criteria. Unless and until we can put forward additional criteria in clear and concrete forms it seems likely that a certain scepticism and confusion in Western countries is likely to continue. Much of the best talent—literary and intellectual—is at present anti-science, anti-industry, anti-technology, and the influence of this viewpoint is far from diminishing.

Of course it can be argued that Britain's position does not give much scope for non-economic objectives and that we must concentrate single-mindedly on high production. Such an argument has been put forward often enough before—for example early in the last century when it was claimed that the rising pressure of foreign competition at that time did not permit the luxury of a shortening of the hours of child labour.

---

* A minor example which may be mentioned at this point is the extension of the shift system—which the British Employers' Confederation wishes to extend still further. (*The Times,* April 24th, 1958.) Because companies are installing more and more complex and costly machinery it becomes increasingly uneconomic to operate except continuously over the whole of the twenty-four hours. Thus it would appear that an ever increasing number of families—and eventually no doubt over the whole world—must adapt themselves to the life of shifts. It is not because they prefer to work like this but rather because, when the economic is regarded as paramount, the shift system appears as an economic necessity. Fortunately the worker still has the opportunity to choose his employment—provided always that the level of employment is high enough to allow him to choose freely.

Economic realism always deserves the greatest respect—and yet almost everything that has been new in Western society, almost every kind of worthwhile reform, has been brought about against " realism's " opposition.

A vigorous economy remains immensely important and especially to Britain under existing conditions. Without it the country would lose much of its zest, as well as its livelihood. But we must learn how to combine two different things which are not incompatible: the first is an expanding economy with all that it means by way of physical well-being; the second is an outlook in industry and commerce responsive to the other forms of well-being not measurable as goods, services or money.

In short, the expectation on which this essay is based is that the industrialized world as a whole will move gradually (as consumer requirements become more fully satisfied) towards a rather changed idea of what an industrial civilization should be; and this not for economic reasons but rather from a realization of the limitations in the economic viewpoint itself, as it has dominated capitalist and socialist theory alike.

Shall we not conclude that our universities and colleges would do something of immense value if they could produce men and women having a new kind of comprehensiveness of outlook on industrial affairs and having the ability to lead industrial society into a new phase? And may it not be that one of the requirements is the more widespread study of economics itself (for example by scientists and engineers)—a study designed to show both the strength and the weakness of economics, and the fact that the presuppositions and value judgments which must be adopted before economics can be applied, have changed considerably during recorded history?

CHAPTER III

CONSUMERS VERSUS PRODUCERS

A Wrong Turning?

ONE of industrialism's most difficult problems—and one where a change of outlook is now most needed—concerns the amount of meaning the employed man can find in his work. What should employment be to a person apart from necessity? At present for the great majority, *i.e.* the men and women in factories, employment amounts to little else than that—little else that is to say than wages. It has been one of the anti-social aspects of industrialism that the character of much of the work which is offered—and especially in mass production—is such that it can be to the worker only so many hours of tedium resulting in so much pay.

Yet wherever there is boredom with work there one finds dissatisfaction and social unrest. Surely it should be one of the important functions of industry in society that the employment it gives should be such that a man can put into his work a great deal of himself. Professional people take it for granted that their own work is of this kind. Must it be assumed that it is contrary to the very nature of the factory system, as it has developed, for the rest of the working population to obtain any comparable sense of achievement? And if this is really the case, shall we not say that the industrial revolution marked something of a wrong turning—or in this respect at least?

But that is perhaps to prejudge the issue—and first it should be said, to avoid misunderstanding, that in almost all other respects industrialism has clearly been of immense benefit to the worker. As well as raising him far above poverty, it has been the means of a vast increase in the scope of education and has also greatly increased the choice of trade and the possibility of travel. The worker's life before modern industry may have been more meaningful, but it was infinitely more restricted.

But these gains are not all. Another is that there is now a much larger fraction of the population who need not be workers (using the term in the accepted sense). Each child has a much greater chance than ever before of finding himself eventually in a profession. As compared to non-industrial conditions, a technical economy requires a much larger number of professionals and a relatively smaller number of manual workers. " White collars " may soon outnumber " grey collars " and quite rightly. Also it is quite erroneous to say—as one hears it said so often—that there are no longer any craftsmen under modern conditions. Those who make this complaint clearly do not know where to find them. For as well as the very large number of those who still are craftsmen in the traditional sense of being skilled with their hands, there is the considerable and still increasing number of those who are craftsmen in the modern sense of being skilled with their brains. Many of those who, before there was a large middle class, would have become societies' artizans, now become dentists, scientists, nurses, engineers, secretaries, and so on—and these are craftsmen in the best sense of the word. Where previously they would have worked directly with their hands (you and me, my reader, in all likelihood!) they now take professional training of all kinds—tens of thousands a year on the scale on which craftsmanship, in this sense, is now practised.

In brief, what these aspects of industrialism amount to is an immense increase in the range of choice; and also, when seen in a different way, to a great increase in certain kinds of responsibility. In a complex society where decisions and actions having long chains of consequences are taken by a large number of people, there is a great demand for the kind of responsibility in the working life—the belief in accuracy, care and expert knowledge—that goes by the much maligned name of professionalism. " It may be," writes D. G. Christopherson, " that this is the most marked of the social effects of technology, that it calls for a huge extension of the attitude of mind formerly associated more or less exclusively with the professions."[1]

So much to the good and if that were the whole story we might well feel content with the purposes of the industrial order as they have been mainly conceived so far. But the actual situation is much more complicated. Industrial societies everywhere are the scenes of great social and personal tensions. Despite all advances the manual workers continue to have a deep-seated sense of servitude and injustice; whilst from the other side the employers, and the professional classes generally, accuse the unions of restrictive practices leading to the holding back of production.

Many of the underlying causes are outside the scope of this essay, but one of them is not and that is the effect of the productive system, as it exists, on the amount of interest and satisfaction obtainable by the worker from his labour. The early industrialists who created industry in its modern form had little idea that it *should* provide interest and satisfaction to those who work in it.* Such a conception, even as a subordinate aim, was entirely foreign to the idea of industry as it grew up in the 18th and 19th centuries. The result has been the lack of concern and responsibility still shown by industrialism for the character of the employment it provides. Industrialism regards it as if it were natural that immense

---

* For example, according to Andrew Ure " . . . on the automatic plan, skilled labour gets progressively superseded, and will eventually be replaced by the mere overlookers of machines." (*The Philosophy of Manufactures*, p. 20, London, 1835.) Though this has not turned out entirely true in detail, it was a correct enough indication of how the industrial attitude towards man and his work was to develop.

numbers of men and women and young people have a working day which quite insufficiently absorbs their interests and offers them no real centre to their lives other than wages.

However, I do not want to assert that " work satisfaction " has necessarily diminished and it would be very difficult to prove that it has. (The division of labour existed long before the modern factory system.) A much more defensible assertion concerns the *meaningfulness* of work and by this I mean its significance in a man's whole life, rather than the satisfaction he may obtain from it during each hour or day. With the growth of the modern system of production (changing the working man into another person's employee), and with the later development of mechanization, it seems likely that meaningfulness in this sense has greatly declined. Arduous and ill-paid though his toil may have been, the pre-factory worker may well have said " This is my life " and have been reasonably content with it. But how many in the factories can say this at present? To a large number of workers the hours in the factories are an annoyance to be escaped from as quickly as possible. What meaningfulness they find in the working life is not in the work itself but rather in the sense of solidarity with their fellows—a solidarity which manifests itself in the union and in the periodic drama of the strike.*

But of course this is not to deny that there have been important advances in other directions: there are now far shorter hours in the factories, much cleaner conditions and less physical fatigue. It is only in regard to the important aspect of work which has been referred to, its quality as meaning and personal fulfilment, that there is no evidence of advance. And indeed industry as a whole is not interested

---

* How does one find out what is in fact an entirely true statement on these matters? Few if any *bona fide* workers have analysed their attitudes in print; few if any sociologists have actually done any manual work in the factories. My own interest in the problem is based on some months of shift work, learning to do various process workers' jobs. Perhaps the best personal account of repetitive work is that of Simone Weil who spent about a year as a worker in the Renault and other factories (*La Condition Ouvrière*, Gallimard, Paris).

and regards the absence of this quality as if it were inevitable and part of the natural order.

Work as Output

What are the factors which have caused this? One of the early industrial assumptions was that the entire object of work is production, that labour has meaning only in terms of its output. This idea has become so much a part of our period's philosophy that it is difficult almost to conceive that any other could exist. And of course the real views of earlier periods on this matter are hard to determine. Yet here and there one finds indications of an earlier conception of work rather different from that which we inherit from the 18th and 19th centuries. Before the advent of industrialism an important Christian influence held that work should play a serious part in the formation of mind and character; that it should, as Richard Baxter put it, "employ the faculties of the soul and body."[2] No doubt this doctrine was not always lived up to: yet it had the social sanctions behind it and was implicit in the master's obligations to his apprentice. In most pre-industrial social theory the idea of the well-being of the worker had some real substance.

With the development of the intensely commercial outlook of the 18th and 19th centuries this was no longer the case. The coming of the new industrial philosophy of work meant that the notion of mutual obligation was replaced by a new conception based on the market. Most men had become other men's employees and they were regarded as selling their labour: labour in exchange for wages. From this it was but a small step to a complete dichotomy of production and consumption—and thereby to an outlook which took little interest in *how* goods were produced so long as they were produced, an outlook which set little store on man's role as a producer and a great deal of store on his role as a consumer.

Our industrial affairs are still like that, but of course there is an important class difference. Millions of " working " men are still employed on a hire and fire basis, and are liable to be laid off as trade conditions seem to require; in short, their labour is regarded as a commodity. This is very far from how the professional classes, and the middle classes generally, think of work as it applies to themselves; indeed they would regard it as quite intolerable.* But as it concerns the working man the whole idea of work has come to be thought of since the industrial revolution in a very negative fashion; not as something which is creative and fulfilling, and which is capable of inspiring a sense of service, but only as so many hours purchased by the employer. This may be called the commodity theory of labour.

In any effort of production it is, of course, the product which is the immediate objective and this is true of all forms of creative activity. Yet the idea that work, if it is treated in the right manner, can have an intensely personal meaning as well is quite alien to the way in which management, even modern management, looks at the matter in relation to its own workpeople. Almost nowhere in large scale industry can one see much recognition that the worker is anything more than a means. Though he is so essential to production he counts for almost nothing in it. Innumerable studies have been carried out on working conditions, on the effects of noise, lighting and so on—almost all without exception have been concerned with the effect on output and almost none with whether or not the worker obtains any real sense of achievement from what he does.

Most managers, when the matter is put to them, agree that much factory work is repetitive and tedious, but they claim that this particular problem is solving itself through the

* The absurdity will be more apparent when it is considered that a man who may have done responsible work as a craftsman for a company for thirty years is still a " hand " and is liable to be laid off, while his daughter, who is a typist with the same company, is " staff-grade ".

progressive reduction of hours. Yet the elimination of tedium, important though it is, is not the most essential part of the problem as it is here envisaged: this is rather how a person's work can become significant and important to him, something round which he can build a large part of his life.

Without this kind of feeling there can be no real will to work and this is obviously harmful to the community, as well as to the individual. And harmful also to the particular firm. Therefore it is surprising that the current view of industrial relations has gone little beyond "incentives".* Any idea of the dignity of work, or of responsibility and service, has been largely excluded by the kind of economic straight-jacket into which almost all industrial thinking has been compressed. When the theory of industrial relations is so much impoverished, so much governed by purely monetary conceptions, it is not surprising that the worker reacts with the same ideas and regards his work as being only so much pay to be earned as easily as he can. Yet it is just that kind of theory which continues to be propagated in many of the standard textbooks on management. And in so far as these books are used in the training of potential managers, the commodity theory of labour remains as a prevailing idea almost throughout industry.

Wherever "management" is studied, whether in the universities or in the Colleges of Technology, the answers to important questions need to be thought out: Can management in the Second Industrial Revolution achieve an outlook on man's work which would see it as something very much more than a mere item of cost? Can the theory of manage-

---

* Concerning incentives in general it is surely an indication of sanity in society that so many people put up a resistace against them. One kind of work may be preferred to another in spite of monetary inducements to the contrary. Good wages did not make coalmining a popular occupation (when it was in demand) and in the universities large numbers of students are still attracted to the arts subjects. The determination of individuals to ignore the attractions of higher incomes and instead to take up whatever occupations please them seems entirely admirable.

ment be remade to show work as having honour and respect in its own right? Of course this is not to say that "cost consciousness" is not very important (teachers of engineering like myself seek to convey its importance continually); what does need to be said is that costs are not the whole story and that whenever an industrial decision involves a change in the manner of work, or other human conditions, this fact needs to be fully brought out and considered.

Meaning and Satisfaction

Looking at the matter more analytically, there are evidently several related problems: the meaningfulness of the actual task; the extent to which the worker in office or factory can achieve a sense of unison with the organization's general purpose; the degree to which he can comprehend this purpose within the life of the whole community.

One of the real difficulties is the extent of specialization. Our society has become highly endowed with advanced techniques of which only a minority of people—those who take some form of technical qualification—can hope to achieve real knowledge. This means that, where the work is highly technical, the non-qualified employees may have little feeling of taking part effectively. The boy or girl whose talents have been insufficient to take him to a grammar school or technical college, and who knows full well that he will end up in a tedious blind alley job, is at the opposite end of the meritocracy to the engineer.

Many of the writers on industrial psychology have concentrated on "work satisfaction" as something more readily attainable than the kind of complete meaningfulness which has been discussed. Two main forms of satisfaction have been suggested[3] : —

(1) The sense of achievement obtainable from the work itself and also the esteem obtainable from others as the result of good work.

(2) The satisfaction obtainable from a feeling of solidarity within a working group, *i.e.* from work as a social activity, the status and security it gives and quite apart from its intrinsic quality.

As remarked earlier, there is no reliable information on how the factory system has affected either of these. One can only speculate. As regards the second, it may be that the advent of relatively small factories marked a gain, as compared to the previously existing cottage industry. The latter is too readily seen as something idyllic—the self-employed craftsman surrounded by his family—and this is to neglect the restrictedness of the life. The effect of the small factory was to enlarge the circle of acquaintances, or at least for the men. Some of the best employer-employee relationships are still to be found in small concerns however decrepit are their premises. But the factory of many thousands is a different matter. Here it may be that the circle has become too large and has the effect of oppressing the employee with the sense of being a " cog in the machine "—as many of them put it.

Repetitive Work

Turning now to the other form of satisfaction, what can be said of the character of work itself, and especially as it exists in factories, as distinct from shops, offices, etc.? Among many of the commentators[4-9] on modern industrialism it has naturally been the repetitive sub-divided task which has been the main object for criticism. Of course not all factory work is of this kind, but a good deal of it is and this is likely to continue. Yet it should be said that neither the division of labour nor the methods of mass production are particularly novel features of modern industry. The former is of great antiquity[10] and the latter, often regarded as late 19th century techniques, were certainly in use a good deal earlier—although on a very restricted scale. They were in use, for example, for the large scale production of ships' biscuits at the Navy Victualling Office at Deptford.[11]

The techniques of the assembly line and the conveyor belt, as developed by Henry Ford and others, were thus the logical conclusion to already existing ideas. Ford said of his factory: "The man who puts in a bolt does not put on the nut; the man who puts on the nut does not tighten it." And he continued: "The net result of the application of these principles is the reduction of the necessity for thought on the part of the worker . . ." As a result of the technical perfection of his foundry ". . . 95 per cent. are unskilled, or to put it more accurately, must be skilled in exactly one operation which the most stupid man can learn within two days."[12]

The psychological and social effects of this type of work have been analysed in great detail by Friedmann.[8] Considering first the more intelligent type of worker, the result of the repetitive task is a more or less continuous state of tiredness due to boredom. The greater the technical perfection of the process the smaller is the likelihood of anything interesting taking place. Thus the effect of technical perfection is to eliminate that kind of eventfulness in the daily life which most people depend on as giving scope for thought and feeling, and the material for remembrance and conversation during leisure.

The tedium of such work—the repetition of the same five or six simple movements which Simone Weil has compared to the tick-tock of a clock—is accentuated by the lack of any sense of achievement. To make anything wholly oneself is to accomplish something. There is no such satisfaction in many forms of mass production. Here during a few seconds or minutes the worker carries out a single operation on a component which then moves forward on the conveyor. The labour takes on a quality of aimlessness. Of course various remedies have been proposed and tried out: against tedium, the rotation of workers between the various tasks; against the sense of nothing achieved, allowing the identical components to accumulate in a pile; against the feeling that the work is without meaning, courses of lectures on each stage in relation to the whole. According to Friedmann, the use of these methods can have useful results, increasing the self-respect of the worker and the quality and quantity of his output. At the same time they are not much more than palliatives; they do not get to the root of the problem as it affects the type of worker who is capable of something better.

Yet there is a second type of worker to whom repetitive work eventually becomes acceptable. This is the kind of man or woman who is able to dissociate his thoughts from his actions—that is to say, the passive worker whose repetitive movements become a reflex action not engaging his higher nervous centres and who does his work whilst day-dreaming. Friedmann quotes many instances of workers who carried out the same simple operation for years on end and who strongly resisted any suggestion that they should move from one such job to another. He has also remarked on the loss of the willpower and the resultant inability to tackle a different job, even at the same conveyor belt.

Of course these are by no means new features of industry. Adam Smith, it will be remembered, had remarked *a propos* of the division of labour that the worker loses the habit of initiative and intelligence and " becomes as stupid and ignorant as it is possible for a human creature to become."[13]

The extent to which these forms of work are deserving of criticism on general social grounds (though they are so important economically), may be looked at from two opposing points of view. On the one hand, Ford was surely entirely right when he claimed that by adapting his processes to the least intelligent he gave them the opportunity for a standard of living otherwise beyond their abilities. The use of mass production, making goods available to the millions, has been the means for great improvements in living conditions and especially for the least able sections of the population. These sections, who in earlier centuries no doubt would have perished, have been enabled to earn their living through the development of forms of work not exceeding their powers.

On the other hand, it seems likely that economic pressures have forced a great many workers into repetitive labour who would have been capable, had the productive system been different, of something a great deal better. There are also the possible genetic effects to be considered. If repetitive work became the normal lot of man over a great many generations it seems likely that it would result in producing, by natural selection, a strain of humans best able to withstand the tedium. Obviously enough such forms of work are quite different in character—far more passive, requiring much less initiative—than those by which man, over a million years, has reached his present stature.

Automation

How does the advent of automation[14] affect what has been said? It may be that automation will be the means of humanizing the factory conditions, as has sometimes been claimed, or it may be that this is to express the matter a little too hopefully. What can surely be said with some confidence is that the more extensive use of fully automatic machinery should reduce the need for repetitive work in many industries and thereby it will reduce the extent to which the worker is subject to the machine.

In the chemical industry automatic control has already been very widely adopted, but primarily for the purpose of reducing costs and obtaining closer control over the quality of the product. From the worker's point of view the result has been to eliminate a great deal of manual operation and in many chemical factories the work of the typical operative has become sedentary and passive. In such factories the instruments which measure temperatures, pressures, etc., are brought together in a control room and these instruments themselves are able to control and rectify the variations in the process through the mechanism of " feed-back ". The work of the control room operative is mainly that of a watcher —except on the rare occasions when the automatic control breaks down and calls for some positive action on his part. At the same time, because he is now one of a much smaller number, he may have much closer contact with management and this may increase his sense of participation in the running of the plant.

The trend in the engineering industry seems to be in a similar direction. The new style of operative is one who keeps an eye on a number of machines working automatically (with automatic transfer of material from one such machine to another) and is called upon only occasionally to rectify some fault in the otherwise smooth running of the system.

In such factories the interesting forms of work are provided not so much by the process of production as by the engineering maintenance which is involved in the upkeep of the plant and of the automatic control apparatus itself. It is at least one very satisfactory aspect of automation that an increasing proportion of the total labour force is now finding employment in these " service " aspects of industry—and also, of course, in the so-called service industries themselves.

The extension of automatic methods to ever larger sections of industry may be expected to be fairly slow. The technical difficulties are considerable and, whenever it is adopted, it requires a vast outlay of new capital and the scrapping of much of the existing plant. Also, there are good grounds for saying that it should be slow. The effect of automation is greatly to reduce the number of workers required for a given output; if it were adopted at a rate greater than the general expansion of the economy it would undoubtedly lead to unemployment. But even when workers can be absorbed in other forms of activity they have to retrain in new and un-usual skills and this may be very hard on the older man whose adaptability has diminished with his years.

But slow or fast, automation is certainly something that is coming. Society's requirements of standardized goods—pots and pans, wireless sets and cars—should eventually be cap-able of production by a much smaller number of men than at present. This will require a re-deployment of the working population and perhaps a further shortening of hours. In so far as automation frees the worker from a subjection to the machine, its coming is surely to be welcomed. Whether or not it will lead to any increase in the meaningfulness of work, or its satisfaction, is a rather different question. Many of the alternative forms of work, whilst they are incapable of being made fully automatic, are nevertheless becoming more impersonal. The best that we can expect of automation is that it will gradually release from the repetitive sub-divided task a great many whose abilities go beyond it. These may be expected to find re-employment in work which is partially or completely mechanized (but is not repetitive) and which may offer greater opportunities for intelligence and initiative.*

So much to the good, but by their very nature there are no forms of mass production which can bring the element of personal creativeness into work. As Erich Fromm re-marks[15]: "Is the hope for effortless work not a daydream based on the fantasy of laziness and push-button power, and a rather unhealthy fantasy at that? Is not work such a funda-mental part of man's existence that it cannot and should never be reduced to almost complete insignificance? Is not the mode of work in itself an essential element in forming a person's character?"

---

* Indeed there is the converse problem of whether there will be *enough* work for those whose abilities are poor. There is the possibility that many of the least able will become engaged in an exhausting economic competition with machines whose productive efficiency is greater than their own.

What Can Be Done?

During the past hundred years or more, social well-being has come to be understood mainly in terms of the supply of goods. This is a conception of well-being quite different from that which had been used in earlier centuries. No doubt its very restrictedness has been a factor which has helped in the building up of the productive system. Yet, in view of the high living standards we have now attained, there is the scope for a broader interpretation and a widening of objectives.

One such line for social advance is surely to tranform the working day into something which is satisfying in itself, as well as being productive. We should regard some part of the sum total of " well being " as meaning the pleasure and dignity of work, and the interest and self-respect of the worker. Whether or not this can be attained in practice may well depend on our ability and willingness to modify assumptions on the economy which have become deeply ingrained. It is the concept of capitalism that capital employs labour, rather than that labour employs capital. Thus man becomes the servant of money. Meanwhile from the side of socialism much less attention has been given to man's working life, and to his life as an individual in society, than to the idea of state ownership. Thus man becomes the servant of the state.

Yet how conditions can be altered so that the average industrial worker will attain a real sense of meaning and consummation in his work is clearly one of the most difficult of modern problems. The gaining of information and the carrying out of social experiments seems the only possible line of approach.

Friedmann, confining his proposals to industry's existing framework, believes that a partial solution is to be looked for in an extended system of apprenticeship training, such as is being developed in France in the Centres d'Apprentissage.

In these schools the aim is not simply technical training but also to help the apprentice to develop himself as a person. In so far as this is a contribution to the present problem, the teaching provides the worker with a better understanding of his particular task in relation to the overall function of the factory; also it gives him a better opportunity, by virtue of general training, to move from one such task to another.* Beyond this Friedmann sees it as an important means of helping the worker to make good use of his leisure by giving him the all-round technical interests which help him to take up home craftsmanship.

Yet the fact that Friedmann, despite the immense scope of his enquiries, should have to put his main hope in what is clearly only a partial solution of the problem, is an indication of the very great difficulty of achieving a complete solution within the existing structure of industry.

Far more radical ideas have been put forward by Lewis Mumford and Simone Weil. Before referring to these it should first be said—and perhaps this is obvious—that different forms of factory system can be thought of as lying at various points between the two extremes: one is the exist-ing kind of system where productive efficiency is the main criterion; the other would be some quite different type of system which might have lower efficiency (and might require longer hours of work if the volume of output were to be maintained) but having as its criterion the quality of the working day.

Many may think that the first of these is closer to the realities of human nature, with its long record of invention for the purpose of increasing output. Yet the failure of so

---

* This is obviously important for quite different reasons. For example, Le Gros Clark has described the difficulty which has been experienced among furniture workers; the difficulty of finding them alternative forms of employ-ment when, towards the end of their working life, *they still know only one task in the factory* and technical change has rendered this task redundant. (*Nature*, 1958, Vol. 181, p. 744.)

many incentive schemes shows that other motives *are* important. It is therefore along the lines of the second criterion that much of the more radical thinking has been active. Mumford,[16] for example, has proposed that whenever it is a question of deciding which of two or more alternative industrial processes should be adopted, the decision should be based not simply, as at present, on the costs but also on the relative amounts of well-being, in the fullest sense, which these processes offer to the employee.

"When we begin to rationalize industry organically, that is to say, with reference to the entire social situation and with reference to the worker himself in all his biological capacities—and not merely with reference to the crude labour product and an extraneous ideal of mechanical efficiency— the worker and his education and his environment become quite as important as the commodity he produces. We already acknowledge this principle on the negative side when we prohibit cheap lead glazes in pottery manufacture because the worker's health is undermined by their use; but it has a positive application as well. Not merely should we prohibit work that is bad for the health: we should promote work that is good for the health."

Somewhat similar views and proposals, involving drastic changes in the organization of industry and methods of production, were put forward by Simone Weil, the French theologian who had worked at the bench in the Renault and other factories. "Up to now, technicians have never had anything else in mind than the requirements of manufacture. If they were to start having always present before them the needs of those who do the manufacturing, the whole technique of production would be slowly transformed. This ought to be part of the instruction given in engineering schools and technical schools generally—but a part with some real substance to it."[17]

4

Her proposals for the reform of the industrial system go a good way beyond this. What she proposes is a far-reaching decentralization of the whole fabric of production. She believes that a great deal of the engineering industry could be dispersed into the countryside and carried out directly on the premises of the individual worker. This would apply, for example, to the production of various small components such as require the use of one machine only. She envisages this machine transferred to the domestic premises of the worker. Only the assembly of the various small components to form the finished product would need to be carried out in a factory. For the rest the proposal is that of a cottage industry, but with the use of modern machines fed by electric power.

Is a scheme of this kind ever likely to be adopted? In India Gandhi's ideas for a decentralized cottage industry were superseded by Nehru's plans—more realistic for the immediate relief of poverty—for a Western style factory system. Yet in the Western world itself a large volume of production has already been attained; if security also can be achieved, together with relief from the pressures of competition, it may be that there will come a demand from the workers' side for the kind of decentralization proposed by Simone Weil; *i.e.* a demand for the conditions of life of the smallholder or shopkeeper, the pleasure of earning his living with his family on his own premises in his own time.

Yet this should come spontaneously if it comes at all. And indeed one of the greatest difficulties in the whole problem is to avoid the kind of paternalism which seems intrinsic to proposals like those of Mumford and Simone Weil. Any realistic solution must be one which comes from the workers themselves, and not from social philosophers or from the state. No other kind of solution would be genuine.

So far the unions have not taken up the matter very actively; they have been far more concerned with wages and hours than with satisfying forms of employment. This does not mean that the problem is not real; it means that it has hardly yet been imagined that factory work and the factory system could be anything other than they are: *the alternatives are not available to be tested.* Almost all organizations for production have evolved simultaneously in a parallel manner—towards largeness, impersonality and a greater degree of division of labour—and the alternatives do not exist. But of course people can only find out what they really want if they have alternatives to choose from, and this provides one of the sound defences of the competitive system in regard to man's role as a consumer. In regard to his role as a producer, *i.e.* concerning his desires on how he should work, very little information is yet available. This can be obtained only by social experiment, by the setting up of " pilot scale " trials of alternative forms of industrial organization; for example, of self-organizing work teams involving a greater devolution of responsibility in the factories[18]; or perhaps more ambitiously of organizations on the lines of the Communautés de Travail which were established after the war in France.[19]

This is not to say that useful changes could not also be made within the existing pattern of industry. The adoption of conditions giving greater scope for initiative in the actual work, together with the extension of " staff-grade " conditions of employment and the attainment of a much greater flow of information from above (such as is reported to exist in Russian factories), might go some way towards attaining among workers a stronger sense of taking part in a responsible fashion. In Britain the " labour force " has been traditionally conceived on almost military lines—so much so that in one well-known British company many of the older members of management still talk about officers, N.C.O.s and men. This should come to an end.

But if it cannot be foreseen in what varieties of ways the problem will be solved, its existence needs to be more widely realized and more extensively discussed. The engineers and managers who control the processes of production enjoy their work and would not wish it to be any less arduous and demanding than it is; what we must surely progress away from is a type of industrial system in which the work available for the millions is often of a quality below their true abilities and where many react by doing as little as possible.

In short, it may be suggested that it is not the " problem of leisure " which faces our society so much as the problem of work. To speak of automation, etc., as creating a problem of leisure, though true enough in a certain sense, is to think of it in the wrong terms. Most people need an outlet for purpose and constructive effort and this is most naturally found in " work ", as it is normally understood. Work implies some effort of the will, some resistance to be conquered. Also it has greater psychological significance than leisure, being related to the means of survival. To think of the matter in terms of the " better use of leisure " is therefore largely to miss the point—that work of some kind (and this *can* include the constructive use of leisure) is for most people almost a psychological necessity.

And as well as being needed by individuals, it is needed by society as a whole. When the situation is widespread that work is tedious and unsatisfying, and provides little release for the emotions, some of the contributory causes of social unrest and delinquency are surely present[20].* As Simone Weil remarks: " Nulle societé ne peut être stable quand toute une catégorie de travailleurs travaille tous les jours, toute la journée, avec dégout."[21]

Yet here again, looking at the problem from this angle, there is the danger of approaching it too much from the

---

* It would be of great interest to study the psychology of strikes from this point of view.

standpoint of the reformer. The whole desirable idea of work as service, as obligation, as fulfilment, appears as being not easily compatible with the forms of economic and political system most favourable to personal freedom. In looking for the kind of solution which will not destroy this freedom the Western countries have an important opportunity. Their people's strong attachment to work is needed if their competitive strength is to be maintained. Yet, looking beyond that aspect of the matter, there will surely come a time when the world will want some new kind of productive system—one which will yield, as well as the output of goods, more rewarding conditions in their making.

CHAPTER IV

THE PARADOX OF RESOURCES

Consumption Separated from Production

" WE shape our buildings," said Churchill, " and afterwards our buildings shape us." And of course he would agree that there is more to it than buildings; it is a question of the man-made surroundings as a whole.

Can it be claimed that industry has done well in how it has shaped us through its influence on the environment? Should it not be said that much of what industry has done has been anti-social, in this respect no less than in regard to the character of the work it has offered? Almost wherever industry built factories, mines and industrial housing during the last century, there it created ugliness, soot and squalor. To be sure, many of the mills and warehouses were actually well designed and were early examples of the " functional " in the best sense. Yet what followed, once the buildings were up, was a complete lack of concern. Industry went about its work chaotically and haphazardly, making an environment of tumult and disregard.

That so much of the industrial residue of the last century still exists and is still lived in is appalling. A railway journey through the industrialized areas of Lancashire and Yorkshire or the Black Country shows clearly enough that an industrial development in the hands of interests which were completely oblivious of all considerations of appearances and treated all matters of amenity, or even ordinary hygiene, as if they were trivial and worthless, has resulted in what continues—continues at the present time—to be nothing less than a scandalous degradation.

In those areas it is not only the smoke and dirt, and the absence of anything whatever that is good to look at, that is so shocking; it is also the aura of spoliation and decay, and the presence of vast numbers of derelict industrial installations which the owners do not take the trouble to dismantle: a landscape of disused collieries, stagnant workings, tumble-down sheds and refuse dumps. As Sartre observes in one of his plays, we make our own hells. Or rather, in this instance, we allowed the 19th century industrialists to do it for us.

Already by 1829 Robert Southey had given a clear warning of what was going on: ". . . the new cottages of the manufacturers (*i.e.* workmen) are . . . upon the manufacturing pattern . . . naked, and in a row. How is it, said I, that everything which is connected with manufacture presents such features of unqualified deformity? . . . Time cannot mellow them; Nature will neither clothe nor conceal them; and they remain always as offensive to the eye as to the mind."[1]

If we ask how all his happened, the answer must be looked for in the social and commercial philosophy of the 18th and 19th centuries. It was a period during which the rights of property were absolute. The ownership of land entitled a man to do anything with what he owned—to put up a colliery here, a row of workmen's houses there and a tip-heap in the distance. And it was a period which believed, for better or for worse, in almost unrestrained freedom for the operations of commerce. All previous control had been left behind and the industrialist could do everything with the utmost speed, in the most makeshift fashion, wherever it led to profit. Business had taken up a sacrosanct position. It had become an almost self-sufficient activity in the interests of which nearly anything could be justified.

Yet there were additional factors which were peculiar to Britain and which may provide the reasons why its industrial environment developed even more offensively than abroad. One of these was the tendency towards a geographical separation of the centres of production and consumption, *i.e.* a segregation of those classes of society which mainly produced from those which mainly consumed, and their use of quite distinct areas of the city for residence, or different cities. The towns where wealth was created were Manchester, Leeds, Sheffield and the like. Of course many of these had well-to-do suburbs, remote from the factories, yet the chief places where wealth was spent were the West End, Cheltenham and Bath. . . . And also the great houses in the shires. For a second and closely related factor, even more characteristically English, was the tradition of the country gentleman. To many of the great industrialists the symbol of success *par excellence* was the building of the country house and participation in the nearby fox-hunt. Perhaps it would not be unfair to speak of the *absentee industrialist.* " City men and manufacturers," wrote Ashton, "moved to the country, sometimes for the amenities it offered, sometimes as a step to Parliament, but often because they cherished the ambition of ending their days on at least level terms with the squires."[2]

In short, the effect of both factors was the removal of much of the wealth produced by industry from the seat of its production and its transfer to geographically separate areas. The industrial towns themselves were not regarded, as Christopher Dawson has put it,[3] as being provincial capitals but rather as places where money was made, where resources were exploited, for the purpose of grinding out fortunes. As the result the industrialists had little desire to create a fine urban environment, and still less to make attractive, or even hygienic, conditions in the close vicinity of the factories. Rather than tolerating the local taxation needed for public amenities, their whole inclination—based on the English country tradition—was to spend what they obtained from their mills in secluded towns or suburbs, or for the construction of country mansions.*

* The painting by Lowry reproduced as a frontispiece to this book is a useful commentary—a gentleman's house, probably originally in open country, which has been surrounded by industry and rendered unusable by its owners.

No doubt these aspirations towards suburban or country life had certain virtues. Yet their effects have been that the industrial towns of England are more uncouth and uncared for than are to be seen almost anywhere else. Nor indeed did they result in a satisfactory countryside in parts of it which were more useful for coal than for hunting. The still surviving slatternly mining villages of the period show clearly enough that the mine owners who built these villages did not, in any sense, identify themselves with the people for whom they built, but regarded them only as so many workers to be housed and fed.

Technological Structures

Great advances in the concept of industrialism could evidently be made in all matters concerning amenity. What needs to be attained is an outlook on the effects of industry which has a positive and not merely a protectionist character. The notion of the " unspoiled " shows clearly enough that our current outlook is still mainly a negative one—the view that the best that can be hoped for is to mitigate as far as possible a damaging assumed to be inevitable. Here in Britain (far more than on the continent) we are still very far from having that kind of positive conception of industry which would see it, not as a spoiling, but rather as being capable, by its actual presence, of improving the surroundings. The presence of agriculture is a humanization of the natural scene and there is no self-evident reason why the same should not also be achieved by industry.

Engineering structures are often by no means unattractive in themselves. Examples from the eotechnic stage* are the Roman aqueducts and the windmills and watermills of later times. Examples from the present neotechnic stage of industry

* The terms eotechnic, paleotechnic and neotechnic, referring to successive but overlapping stages in the evolution of technology over the past few centuries, are those used by Patrick Geddes (*Cities in Evolution*, Williams and Norgate, London 1949) and by Lewis Mumford (*The Culture of Cities*, Secker and Warburg, London 1940).

are bridges and dams and certain power stations; and also (although these are in a somewhat different category) almost every kind of ship, including the steamship, and again the various kinds of aircraft. What appear as being the conditions which are necessary for the acceptance and appreciation of such structures are: (1) an intrinsic seemliness in their design; (2) the absence of any association with the smoke and squalor of the last century; (3) a generation or more of familiarity with their uses.

These conditions are met by the structures already mentioned and by several others. The lighthouse is an example of a highly technological object which yet has great simplicity of design and no unpleasant associations to detract from its enjoyment. However there are others whose good visual qualities become apparent only when they are seen in the distance, the mess which usually surrounds them obscured from view. Such for example are the tall waterless gas-holders —those delicate green rotundas which, when they are caught sight of over a hilltop, are amongst the most interesting shapes on the London scene.

But all too often it is the mess that spoils everything. It is the general slatternliness of industry about which a great deal needs to be done, much more than to improve the engineering structures. No doubt one of the first steps is to rid ourselves of that abomination of a smoky or dirt laden atmosphere which has been one of the scandals of the factory system. Given greater willingness, the laws against the emission of dense smoke could have been brought into effect a good deal earlier. With the use of smokeless fuel, and more especially with the coming of nuclear energy, it should be possible to achieve clean air in the foreseeable future. And no doubt that would lead on to a great deal of cleaning up and repainting.

Another useful advance would be legislation against industrial litter and decrepit premises. Laws have rightly been passed against the leaving of litter by the public. But as yet there appear to be no laws which would require industry to keep its innumerable rubbish dumps invisible, or laws which would require the dismantlement of broken-down sheds and decrepit collieries, the filling-in of old workings and the removal of disused railway lines; in general the maintenance of conditions of tidiness and good appearance. Obviously this would result in some increase of industrial costs; but in the long term a revitalizing of the environment might be expected to repay the expenditure—and especially in the decaying areas of the North which modern industry tends to avoid.*

The cutting down of unnecessary advertisement would also be a useful step forward and the filling stations are a case in point. The petrol companies are so few in number that it would appear easy for them to reach agreement among themselves to avoid too brash an appearance of their stations—and that without selling a gallon of petrol less. If they would also engage an architect to work out for them a dozen or more quiet designs, suitable for various settings in the towns or open country, this would be indeed a public service.

Apart from the avoidance of mess and unnecessary display, a great deal could also be achieved in regard to the architectural design of the factories themselves, and the layout of industrial premises. So far it has been mainly the power stations which have been thought of as the theme of important architecture. As regards private companies there are many who will put up an imposing office block for prestige purposes, but apparently few who will use an architect to work in association with their engineers for the external design of the manufacturing plant. And there are fewer still who will engage a landscape architect to consider the factory's relationship with its surroundings. Yet what is so clearly needed, and before

---

* This is surely one of the saddest aspects of the whole business. Many are the grimy northern towns which industry no longer wants, preferring to leave them behind for newer sites, more attractive for the recruitment of staff.

any construction takes place, is a visualizing of how the various items of plant can best be made to harmonize with each other, and to harmonize also with the neighbouring landscape. Many technological structures, it has been suggested, are intrinsically attractive; yet in the planning of factories the good visual qualities of the individual items are often lost by putting these items in unsuitable positions relative to each other. In the placing of the masses, in the juxtaposition of the angles of roofs and walls and of the various pieces of plant, and in their relationship to the environment, there is scope for a new kind of architectural achievement.*

That things like this can be done is shown by the example of a Scottish company who chose Sir Basil Spence as their architectural consultant in the lay-out and colouring of their chemical plant†—a type of factory where aesthetic factors had hardly been considered previously. And thus quite generally what is needed is the attitude of mind which believes that certain forms of expenditure are worthwhile, even though they do not raise " efficiency " as it is conventionally understood.

Industry, by spending a little more on its appearance, would help to make a country more enjoyable to live in and more completely alive. Thereby it would serve its own long-term interests as well. In the past it was able to recruit its workers and its staff almost regardless of location. But that is far from being the case at present. The really decisive factor in achieving smoke abatement in Pittsburg, it has been said, was the steel industry's realization that without abatement it

---

* Is it not one of the aims of modern art to show that significant form (to use an older expression) can be obtained by welding together a few pieces of old metal, or by means of newspaper cuttings and other debris of modern life put together as *collage?* And if the artist can express form by use of these modest materials, is this perhaps his unconscious criticism of the industrial order which attains only chaos, though it has such immensely greater resources at its disposal?

† The Scottish Agricultural Industries' fertilizer plant at Leith.

was no longer able to get good staff. Much the same situation occurs in Britain—the companies which are the best magnets are those in the new industrial areas, or in the "non-industrial" towns—Harrogate, Gloucester, Cambridge—which have something pleasant to offer. Moreover the generally greater cleanliness and modernity of most American industrial cities is an important factor in the loss from Britain of engineers and scientists.

A Modern Failure

So far this chapter has been concerned with those parts of the surroundings which are industrial. Obviously enough the influence of industrialism has extended much further afield and, during the past two centuries, it has been the strongest of forces acting on the urban scene in its entirety. The whole quality of living in towns has changed immensely —and of course in several respects for the better: in regard to housing especially it can hardly be doubted that more people are now better accommodated than ever before. Yet it would hardly be going too far to say that the state of our cities is one of the most conspicuous failures of industrialism and, if we are to aim at advancing this form of civilization, the improvement of the cities seems one of the most essential steps.

The feature of the modern city which is most commonly criticized is the state of the streets, the congestion of the traffic. Yet that is perhaps the least of the evils. When the matter is looked at from the standpoint of the vast numbers living in the most densely populated areas the whole problem of the city takes on a much darker aspect. Many slums have been cleared; but there still exist vast areas of squalid and decaying property, the homes of millions, so densely crowded that there is almost no provision for playing fields (a fact we take far too much for granted) or for recreation in the fresh air of any sort. As the result immense numbers of young people are at a loose end in the streets. These conditions, it may be hoped, are a passing phase and will be rectified as wealth increases. Yet our cities based on industrialism are a failure in a further respect and in this there is little sign of impending improvement. This concerns appearance and enjoyment, factors affecting us far more vitally than a utilitarian age is willing to admit. It is part of the paradox referred to in the chapter title that although we have these immense resources of wealth and materials the towns and cities we have made for ourselves are greatly inferior, even in our own eyes, to those still standing from the Middle Ages and the Renaissance.

In the handbooks Venice, Florence and Bruges, and other cities of their time, are now described as " cities of art "; yet to those who built them these were no more than the contemporary centres of industry and commerce. Their counterparts in the world of modern industry are towns such as Birmingham and Manchester, and these were built at a time when far greater resources were available. It is the measure of our poor expectation of what industrialism is capable of achieving that it seems almost ludicrous to suggest that these towns might have been made the equals of Venice or Florence.

Why Britain has been so particularly backward in making fine industrial towns may have had several causes. One of the most important has already been discussed—the social custom whereby those who had wealth chose to spend it in places far from industry. Conversely a factor which helped Germany and Italy towards a better state of affairs was the fact that almost every town of any size was a capital. The autonomous rulers established their courts in the various cities and built their palaces, not in the country, but *at the city centres*. This often resulted in spacious planning—and also a self-supporting culture. Many quite ordinary German towns such as Mannheim and Darmstadt, the seats of such courts, continue to be far more attractive than English cities, for example

Bradford and Oldham, which are comparable in population and industry.

Among the few clear indications of better things in prospect are some of the new town centres such as Stevenage and Crawley. For the rest we seem content to allow our cities to drift from bad to worse. And thus we accept, almost without question, the ugliness, the overcrowding, the congestion of the traffic and the great shortage of amenities, especially of those required for health and interest amongst the largest number.

The Dilemma of Planning

All this leads on to the question of planning, a question which is often thought of as meaning a certain dilemma: shall we remake our environment deliberately or leave its evolution to processes of spontaneous change? But of course it can hardly be said that man-made changes ever occur spontaneously and the real question at issue is better expressed in terms of the idea of scale, *i.e.* as being concerned with how large a part of the environment should be planned as a unit, how many adjacent buildings (each of which we have no doubt should be "planned") should come within the compass of a unifying scheme.

Obviously enough many of the urban areas which are most admired are precisely those which were planned on the large: Paris offers important examples of "state planning" as done by Louis XIV and Colbert*; Edinburgh New Town, Bath and many of the London squares are instances of rather smaller scale planning achieved by private builders.

These English and Scottish examples are from the 18th and early 19th centuries. Some sporadic ideas on large scale planning appeared during the later half of the century and

---

* Le Corbusier goes so far as to describe Louis XIV as the first Western town planner since the Romans. (*The City of To-morrow*, pp. 39 and 260, John Rodker, London 1929.)

were embodied in Saltire, Bournville, Letchworth and Welwyn Garden City. Yet the century as a whole was too individualistic to give much welcome to the idea of extensive planning. It was not until the present forties—the period of the Town and Country planning Act, of the New Towns and the setting up of a special ministry—that comprehensive planning again made appreciable progress. And then only for a very short time. Since the forties, as Professor Matthew has remarked, everything has slipped back: " Planning has now, after gradual demotion among government departments, no longer even a titular appearance. If it has gone in the letter, it has gone even more in the spirit."[4]

This retreat from planning is naturally related to a revived belief in the free play of the market and a minimum of official controls. And it would be idle to deny that this trend corresponds to certain widely felt desires: to resist the growth of too much bureaucracy; to avoid an excessive organization of people in masses, the houses they live in and the forms of their social life; to preserve the openness of society and the diversity of its processes.

And here indeed is the crux of much of the modern dilemma and especially concerning town and country planning. For however desirable it is to avoid an excess of organization, the salient fact of our modern civilization is that it aims at providing for everyone the amenities previously available only to the few. Hence the immense increase in the number of vehicles, the steady growth of the cities, the great expansion of the factory system and the invasion of the landscape by power stations, transmission lines and refineries. All this implies at least some organization and planning if it is not to occur entirely haphazardly and with a great deal of frustration of human effort.

It is thus an immensely important question to what extent a society which rightly resists excessive concentration of power is able to perform those tasks which are now crying out to be done: the rebuilding of large areas in the decaying inner rings; the creation of parks and playing fields and yet more houses; the construction of shopping precincts or two-decker streets; the giving of a new face to the northern towns and the prevention of industrial sprawl over the landscape.

The whole question of the necessary amount of organization of a mass society is obviously immensely complicated: with too little it becomes chaotic and unlivable in; with too much it becomes rigid and mechanical. Considerably more planning may be needed than has yet been accepted. Even so, it may be hoped that we shall not move too far from a somewhat opposing outlook: the need to maintain adequate opportunities for free choice and individual effort, to keep the whole concept of planning at a human scale and containing within it the necessary element of diversity.

Whatever may be the solution to this problem, it seems clear that a real improvement of our cities cannot take place until there is a radical change in the general attitude towards the economic rent, and towards the rates and public expenditure.

Concerning rents, it is known that in Scotland, to take an extreme example, the average for a council house in 1961 was a mere 10/1d. a week[5]—less than many of the occupants were spending on the rental of a television set—and such houses contained more than a third of the Scottish population. If people are unwilling to pay for them, good housing and good cities obviously cannot be attained.

The same applies to the provision of public amenities. In Western countries we are inclined to regard all forms of rates and taxes, even when they result in roads, schools, meeting halls, etc., as if they were a kind of theft. This is partly the result of the deeply ingrained sense of property. It is also the result, as Robbins has remarked,[6] of the fact that under democratic conditions there is a natural presumption in favour of private, as against public, goods since the former are more freely chosen. Having this attitude we run some risk that our provision for the civilized amenities will be overtaken by that which is given in the more highly planned Communist countries.

The example of Germany shows clearly enough that even the very large scale rebuilding of cities can be achieved without excessive difficulty. The magnitude of what was done in the war-devastated towns shows also that it is not the economic aspect that is the main obstacle. The total of an industrial nation's capital in the form of buildings amounts to the value of only a few years of the gross national product. Much of our unsatisfactory urban environment could undoubtedly be replaced in a fairly short time, given sufficient willingness and effort.

And in this connection it may be remarked that a society's outlook is probably greatly affected by the age of the bulk of its capital equipment. Here in Britain much of our housing and a large number of our factories are at least fifty years old —and have no particular merit. Believing that we have to make do, we create a cult—old houses, old cars, even old locomotives. No doubt this is one of the reasons why much of our industry is not progressive. A great renewal of fixed capital, as in Germany after the war, though it is somewhat destructive of tradition, can help immensely to revive national energies.

The real obstacle is surely not so much economic as psychological and is the lack of a willingness to pull down and rebuild and to adopt whatever forms of planning may be needed. The political parties have not yet given this problem the amount of attention it deserves. Towards the putting forward of new objectives for our society, in relation to the whole question of urban living, the parties might now be giving a good deal of thought.

Yet to regard the matter as being entirely one for government would be to think of it too much in terms of state planning. It is also private industry and commerce, by its choice of office buildings, filling stations, factories and so on, which has the power either greatly to spoil the urban scene, or greatly to improve it. At an earlier time great embellishments of the cities were made by merchants and bankers. What is so much needed at present on the part of industrial and commercial leaders is an active state of sympathy—an imaginative grasp of what again they could achieve in the shaping of a civilization by its environment.

CHAPTER V

TRANSCENDING THE MACHINE

A Falling Apart

IN his short story *A Salzburg Comedy*, Erich Kästner remarked that Salzburg is a happy place because it is a place where life and art are not separate but are blended together. In the older European tradition of which he speaks, art is not something to be admired in museums or discussed learnedly in university circles; it is rather that which is found wherever work is done lovingly, where thought is given to detail and there is a wish for perfection. It is to be found in the care of the house or the garden, in craftsmanship, in a person's behaviour and speech and writing. In brief, it shows itself, at least partially, in a sense of style.

Of course this is not everything about art, but art has its beginnings in the everyday life—in the taking of care in order to give pleasure. In English domestic life art is surely present, almost more than anywhere else, in the cultivation of the garden.

But all this seems poles apart from the world of industry. In an earlier chapter it was remarked that the advent of modern industrialism caused a great deviation from the earlier equilibrium in European culture. The immense concentration of attention on the new productive methods gave rise to an attitude to industrial work as meaning no more than output and an attitude to the new industrial centres as meaning no more than the places where output was obtained. Yet if we could now bring that earlier tradition to bear on industry, achieving a great strengthening of the aesthetic impulses in relation to technology and commerce, the whole atmosphere of our society might be greatly transformed.

The Middle Ages and the Renaissance were periods which conceived their technology and commerce in both a narrower and a broader sense than we do at present. Narrower in so far as those periods had little conception of using their resources for a dynamic advance in the ordinary person's living standards; broader in so far as the commercial and artistic life were much nearer together, and technology was regarded as being much more closely related to the arts than it has been since. One example is the cathedrals where engineering attained a fusion with the greatest art to an almost miraculous degree. Another is the paintings of the Dutch masters where we are shown the industrial life as an integral part of the whole. The ships and shipyards, the wind and water mills and other industrial structures were depicted quite unselfconsciously, as if in an accepted state of harmony with the countryside and the towns.

Only mining was regarded as if it were a thing apart (as may be seen in the opening chapters of Agricola's *De re Metallica*) but otherwise there was a strong spirit of integration and especially in the culture of Italy and the Netherlands. In those countries leaders of commerce were active in the commissioning of sculpture and painting, and bankers were engaged in putting up superb architecture in the cities. As Lewis Mumford remarks, "These moments of balance between art and technics . . . represent a high point in any civilization's development."[1]

It is an important question why the kind of industrialism which came to the fore during the 18th and 19th centuries took such a different turning, why technology and the arts parted company and fell away.

A closely related question—why 19th century industry was so regardless of its environment—was brought up in the previous chapter. It was remarked that the leadership of industry had moved from the aristocracy to an almost new middle class; that commercial success had come to be regarded as being almost self-justifying and that no question of amenity could stand out against it; and finally that the towns, or parts of towns, where wealth was made were not the places where wealth was mainly used. These factors all have an important bearing on the present question; yet there were others having the same tendencies and arising more directly from the newly developed methods of production by machine.

It was soon realized that the natural logic of these methods was, at that time, towards quantity far more than towards quality. Such was the demand for goods, from a population which previously had little beyond the bare necessities, that there was little need for any serious study of design. To be sure the products of industry were under criticism from high quarters and in Britain this criticism led to the setting up of the government design schools and the opening of the Great Exhibition. Yet the thoughts of the new industrialists were drawn much more to the profit than to the product. Many were from a yeoman or puritan background and were much less inclined to the arts than had been the commercial leaders of an earlier period.

If the interest in the product did not come from the masters still less did it come from the men. Their entire status had changed during the process of industrialization. Previously many had been creative artizans in their own right, putting their own ideas and craftsmanship into the product. Henceforth they were machine attendants and, although their incomes were rising, the influence they could exert on their products had become far less.

Yet another important factor was the replacement of hedonism by efficiency as an important social criterion. In Western countries this was a significant trend during the 19th and the first half of the 20th centuries. What mattered earlier was refinement of living for a small minority; what came to matter was cheap and efficient production for the whole population. The new criterion, which was partly ethical and gave expression to the social conscience, steadily replaced the earlier one which derived from the cultivated tastes of the few. Probably much more was gained than was lost as the result of this change of outlook. The great artistic achievements of an earlier period had been at the expense of living standards which for the largest number must have been pitiably low. Yet for all that there was a loss; as industrialism advanced the belief in things being of value in themselves, the desire for perfection, the sense of style, all diminished. What took their place was the desire above all for output; and the immense numbers for whom large output was of such inestimable value were not yet ready to form new tastes of their own.

For all these reasons, and perhaps others also, the general effect during the 19th century was a falling apart. The idea of technology became associated with a mainly utilitarian attitude of mind, one which was very different to that which had been natural to Leonardo or to Brunelleschi—or even to Wedgwood as late as the 18th century. Men of the earlier European tradition such as these had brought to their engineering and their arts a synoptic outlook and had formed a conception of technology as being as closely related to the artistic life as it is to the economic. All this was lost during the early period of industrialism.

A Coming Together

More recently, however, there have been hopeful signs that this conception is being somewhat regained and these may be seen in the work of men such as Gropius, Pasmore and Nervi. This movement to achieve greater harmony between industry and the arts extends, of course, in many directions: towards industrial design where the designer, working close to certain ideas of abstract art,[2] aims at the particular shapes most harmonious with production by machine; towards architecture and town planning where so many of the arts and technologies must work in unison; most significantly of all perhaps towards the landscape as a whole. For here there is clearly developing a new idea of landscape architecture—somewhat as it was practised by the designers of the great parks of the 18th century but concerned now with the building of roads, the location of industry and the choice of buildings suited to their surroundings—in brief, with the whole idea of land use in an industrial age.[3]

These various signs that the arts are beginning to exert greater influence on industrial society are surely of immense promise. They show the commencement of a movement whose effects could be far reaching. The enjoyment of painting and music is already more widespread than ever before, and another significant development has been the immense growth in the popularity of home craftsmanship. In the streets of our towns the Civic Trust movement, starting with Magdalen Street in Norwich, has made useful progress towards the removal of clutter and the attainment of more lively colours of shops and buildings. And within industry itself there has been a gradually strengthening idea of its need to be concerned with the visual, as well as with the practical, qualities of its products, and also with the appearance of its factories.

In Holland and Switzerland, less hampered than Britain by the all-pervading relics of the 19th century, there is already the advent of a better kind of industrial milieu. In both countries the electrification of the railways and the reduction of the smoke nuisance have probably been important factors which have encouraged industry to improve itself. Yet it is perhaps in Italy that the coming together of technology and the arts has taken the clearest shape. The average Italian seems to be much less self-conscious about art than is the Britisher or the American and, at the same time, has a kind of natural interest in mechanical devices.

Whatever it may be, the Italians have a happy knack in almost all matters concerning the arts in relation to engineering.

Yet much conscious thought has also been given and Leonardo Sinisgalli has given the whole movement a sense of direction with his journal *Civilta delle Macchine*. A literary magazine such as *Il Menabò* devotes an entire number to the question of literature in relation to industry. The close collaboration of Italian engineers and designers in the production of cars, typewriters, etc., is well known, yet the collaboration appears to be equally effective in the field of building. At the Milan Polytechnic architects and civil engineers have the first two years of their professional training in common. Buildings are often known by the names of their architects and engineers jointly, and not by that of the architect alone. In the culture of Northern Italy as a whole there seems to be a general urge to bring beauty and utility together, the result of a natural inclination towards colour and form, together with whatever science may give that will make life more enjoyable.

The Desire for the Distinctive

If, at an earlier stage of industrialism, efficiency took the place of hedonism as an important social criterion, there are evidently the signs that this trend is now being reversed. Beauty and enjoyment were natural objectives for the dominant few of pre-industrial society; efficiency became important when new means of production and an increasingly democratic outlook combined to make the population as a whole reach out for higher living standards; more recently the aesthetic judgement has again become a significant factor, the result of the basic necessities having become plentiful enough to allow other interests to assert themselves. As Galbraith has remarked, at one stage of industrialism it is the engineering that matters and at a later stage it is the beauty of design of the product.[4]

If this desire for beauty, and the means of satisfying it by a considerable and increasing part of the public, continues to gain strength it might have important effects on the whole pattern of industrial society. The desire in question looks always for what is singular or unique and in this respect its influence is against mechanization. The results could be far reaching and not least in the field of production.

Clearly enough there are two opposing inclinations concerning the kinds of goods which are wanted. One of them is the wish for cheapness. This greatly favours mass production, which gives us a small choice of standardized goods at a low price. The other is the desire for high quality—and also, if possible, for " something different ". This gives rise to a reaction against the mass produced article and results in a growing demand for goods which are far more individual —and this is occurring most noticeably in furniture, textiles and ceramics.

In short, there is an almost universal longing for the distinctive; yet what is more significant is that eventually a large fraction of the population may be expected to have the means of satisfying this desire. If so, it could lead to the demand for an appreciable output of goods which are *individually made* and this would require not only designers but also craftsmen. This means the possibility of an increasing number of workers having satisfying and creative work.

With further increase in wealth there may thus occur a significant shift in the character of employment. And correspondingly in the nature of technical training. As well as training apprentices to work in mass production, our technical schools may be teaching the more gifted or adventurous craftsmen how to develop their own powers of self-expression in design, and how to set up on their own or in co-operative units.

What has just been said is by no means to return to the viewpoint of William Morris and his group. Here there is no question of setting ourselves against the machine. Mechanization is surely to be welcomed for all products whose primary requirement is cheapness or standard quality; for all others the natural desire for variety and individuality may cause us to go beyond it. But of course this is by no means to dispense with the technical aids which are available. ". . . the artist can resist mechanization," remarked Victor Pasmore, "not by reasserting handcraft, but by using the machine and transcending it."

And that, it may be suggested, is the attitude we should adopt quite generally towards the machine. That is to say, to use it where it is useful but always to keep it subordinate. Like other techniques, the machine becomes civilized when it reaches a stage of perfection such that it is no longer demanding and falls into its natural place. If that kind of viewpoint can be achieved it would surely be a useful factor in modifying and improving the whole atmosphere of industrialism.

From this it is not far to conclude that a well-conceived educational policy for the schools would be one which gave an important place to the training of the aesthetic sense, this being the basis of much of what has been discussed. And further that great support needs to be given to the Art Colleges and the schools of industrial design, encouraging them to produce in larger numbers the men and women who would be capable of achieving a real synthesis of technology and the arts.

CHAPTER VI

PUBLIC CONSCIENCE AND PRIVATE UNCERTAINTY

Finding One's Way

THE term " mass society " is used a great deal and most often in a pejorative sense. Yet much of what is meant by " mass " is no new phenomenon but has been taking place for over a century. This applies, for example, to the coming together in the towns of a large industrial proletariat—in Britain the result of the enclosures as well as of the growth of the factories. The " mass media ", in the form of popular newspapers and magazines, have likewise been growing to their present proportions during a century or more. So also has mass production itself.

The term " mass " is clearly a complex of many tendencies —and not all of them by any means are for the worse. It has been mass production which has provided goods for people at prices they can afford. It has been the products of the communications industry, including its new forms television and radio, which have stimulated vast numbers to read and listen. The result has been that many whose school education was poor have nevertheless become much better at expressing themselves and much better informed.

Also this mass society based on industrialism has seen the growth of a strong social conscience and this is surely its best achievement. As well as the belief in the fair distribution of goods, there is the recognition that people must be looked after when they fall ill, when they become old and when they are out of employment—and that all of this, and education too, must be paid for as commonweal. To be sure these forms of welfare are, in a sense, institutional and impersonal; yet our society is also—and in a far more human respect—a much kindlier one than it was only twenty or thirty years ago. For apart from what the state does for the individual there is also a much gentler feeling between one person and another—and the change for the better is especially noticeable as between people of markedly different social class or of personal circumstance. The poor are no longer condemned as ne'er-do-wells; the infirm and the ill are accepted far more for what they are. To a much greater extent than earlier we live as members of one another.

All that is to the good. And yet! . . . There remains a certain sense of disquiet, a feeling that all is not well with industrial societies at their roots. The prevalence of crime and hooliganism is only one of its causes. Another is the existence of a large number of people who are entirely law-abiding and yet are dissatisfied and restless, people suffering from a sense of grievance and frustration, or from the feeling of a lack of meaning in their lives. Industrial societies everywhere are the scenes of a general shiftlessness and the absence of settled purposes. In all of them there is a certain diffused atmosphere of nihilism and disbelief. ". . . the great misfortune, the root of all the evil to come," wrote Pasternak in a somewhat different context, " was the loss of faith in the value of personal opinions."[1]

And thus if industrialism is found associated with a strongly developed social conscience and a real kindliness of spirit, it is also accompanied by a widespread sense of uncertainty and self-doubt, by a state of society in which people find difficulty in achieving firm convictions or a strong sense of personal direction. And although these two facets of industrialism may appear as being somewhat contrary to each other, they surely both derive from a single source—and this is largeness of scale.

Large and Small Scale Structure

It is the largeness of our organizations—factories and offices as well as schools, universities and hospitals—which is the basis of high output, whether this be measured in terms of goods or services. And it is only because output is high, the result of this largeness, that our society (which has otherwise a highly individualistic tradition) is willing to use part of this output for purposes which are altruistic. The possibility of a social conscience, and stemming from that genuine good feeling between people from different backgrounds, is dependent on the existence of organizations large enough to achieve a big volume of production.

Yet it is this same largeness of scale, so beneficial on the material side, which appears as harmful on the psychological. Making the individual smaller, its further effect is to give him a depressed view of his own powers of comprehension. No doubt there are millions who fail to achieve any real intellectual grasp of the workings of their own offices and factories. When people have this feeling of being overshadowed by forces far beyond their understanding they naturally regard it as worse than useless to formulate any opinions of their own. Easier always to move with the stream.

And thus at the heart of the modern situation is a certain anguish: How is one to find one's way in life in this environment of vast organizations and uncomprehended powers? Sculptors such as Lynn Chadwick and Paolozzi have expressed something of the pathos of the human being in his modern surroundings; their figures, dumb and unseeing and put together out of rough pieces of metal, have the sense of being utterly lost and alone.

Relative to most earlier states of Western society, ours is amorphous and fluid and has little or no small scale structure suitable for the individual to hold on to. Most people no longer have the kind of support which is provided by long

residence in the same district; the effect of improved trans-
port and greater social mobility has been to make one's own
locality seem much less of a firm centre. Also the communications industry has developed as the new large-scale structure
of authority and opinion and has mainly replaced the former
small-scale structure based on the community of local church
or village. Yet it has nowhere near the same stabilizing influence. What is said in the newspaper or on the programme
represents the highest common factor for a vast number
whose actual circumstances may differ widely. Opinion itself
has become a mass production product and this is not of
much help to people when they are trying to find a sense
of meaning in their lives or to solve personal problems of
their own. On the glossy pages of the magazines little can
take a firm hold.

Much might be achieved if we could build up a new small-
scale structure round the contemporary centres of interest;
that is to say, round sports clubs, music and drama societies,
and all activities which can create small friendly groups.
Most people have the desire to strengthen their local affilia-
tions and to enter into sociable relationships with others;
voluntary movements in this direction need to be given every
encouragement and to the extent of putting down sufficient
sums of public money; for example, for sports centres whose
facilities could be let out on hire to clubs, and for multi-
purpose assembly halls, such as exist in some of the Danish
towns, for the use of societies.

In general it may be hoped that the "mass society" is
only a transitional stage in the evolution of industrialism.
Though it came into existence as part of the process of creating high living standards, there seems no necessity that the
mass idea should remain with us permanently. One factor
working against it was brought up earlier—the desire for
distinctiveness as leading to a renewed demand for craftsmanship and more generally as offsetting the influence of the

machine. Equally important could be a sociable movement such as has been discussed. Progress beyond the mass society is to be looked for neither by political change nor by still greater efforts at organization (for these would be to accentuate the mass tendencies) but rather in the opposite direction of a strengthening of the social structure on the smallest scale.

Self-Respect and Self-Reliance

A useful contribution could also be made through education. Personal interests need to be awakened early; and for a person to have these interests is not only to make it easier for him to take part in social activities; it is also to have the inner resources he needs in family life and when he is on his own. In the counteracting of those tendencies in industrial society which lead to nihilism and self-doubt, education's part must be to bring out internal powers and independence of mind, and to strengthen those qualities in a person which give him the sense of controlling his own destiny, of knowing where he is going.

Our British educational system does not achieve this very effectively for the great majority. It is a system which does an excellent job for the few—those who go through grammar schools and universities—but a rather poor one for the majority who go through neither. Many of our people are in a poor state of mind and spirit—rough, boorish and having a complete lack of regard for anything that is worthwhile —and more so I think than in other Western countries. This is a state of affairs we take far too much for granted. Our social system is so much wedded to the idea of class and to the idea of levels of behaviour appropriate to class, that the continued existence of what is essentially a low-caste section of the population is regarded almost as if it were natural.

Towards changing this state of affairs, one of the qualities far more of our people need is self-respect. This requires better command of language and a less class-differentiated manner of speech. It requires also an improved working knowledge of our social institutions—laws and regulations and mechanisms of local and national government—something on the lines of what in American schools is called " civics ", *i.e.* the essential information needed to give the future citizen confidence in handling his own affairs.* To a much greater extent than the British, the American educational system creates a sense of respect for the ordinary man; it stands for the idea of the whole electorate, and not just a part of it, being responsible and well-informed.

Equally necessary is the encouragement of self-reliance and this is as important in leisure as it is in work. Much of our modern situation can be understood in terms of contending forces: on the one side are the large organizations creating a pressure of uniformity and making for a loss of faith, as Pasternak puts it, in the value of personal opinions; on the other side are the forces of the self aiming at the safeguarding of its own identity, aiming at keeping intact its liberty of thought and action.

Towards the harmonizing of these forces an important means may be found in the complementary roles of work and leisure; work as providing the occasion for each individual to fulfil himself in relation to society; leisure as giving him the chance, when it is not given by his work, for his own self-realization as a person. During the twenty-four hours each man or woman has the opportunity of living both socially and individually; opportunity, that is, if his work does not exhaust him before leisure and if his education fits him adequately for both.

Of course it may be that leisure will eventually become as highly organized, or as impersonal, as most work is at

---

* This is not to say that the development of the powers of criticism (*e.g.* in relation to what a person reads in his newspaper, what he sees in advertisements, etc.) is not equally important and some of the means of doing this in the schools were described many years ago in Leavis and Thompson's *Culture and Environment* (Chatto and Windus, 1933).

present. If men were to take their leisure *en masse* they would not have much need of the qualities I am referring to. But that seems unlikely—men value their liberty for the freedom it gives, for the ability to be themselves. During work most employees feel constrained, under duress; leisure is the opportunity to exist freely in private. Work and leisure should be such that they are able to satisfy a person in his complementary requirements: on the one side as a member of society having constructive work related to that society; on the other as a person in his own right, a person (as W. R. Niblett[2] puts it) with an independent will and centre.

If this view be accepted it would seem that a guiding idea in education should be this complementarity of the working hours and the leisure hours; education would be simultaneously for social living, which includes work, and for private living.

The needs of the former are probably better understood and catered for than of the latter. Much educational theory gives great emphasis to man's place in society—to his work and citizenship—and it seems entirely sound that it should. Each boy or girl should have it as a right that his education will help him (or her) towards earning a living or making a home; it is ridiculous to suppose that some measure of vocational training cannot be combined with education in the best sense. The understanding of citizenship is also an important aim in education and so again is co-operativeness of outlook which is essential in any social relationship between equals. Yet the needs of leisure are somewhat different. Here the important thing in education is to show a person how he can make the most of his own resources—but more particularly of those resources he can use *when he is on his own*. Everyone needs to have the capacity for existing at least part of the time self-reliant and self-contained.

Countrymen have this capacity and with them it is the result, not of education, but of the simple fact that they are almost always occupied. In an unhurried manner they are continuously busy—if not with work for the employer, with work for themselves. Townsmen, for the most part, do not have this capacity to the same extent; yet the more important becomes the " problem of leisure "—and it is an important problem in spite of what was said earlier about the greater psychological significance of work—the more necessary is self-reliance.

Where does this lead? " The main function of education," wrote John Macmurray, " is to train men and women for freedom, not for work; just as the main business of civilization is to liberate men from the necessity of labour, that they may have leisure to live freely."[3] Without agreeing with this entirely I believe that education should give a great deal of attention to the stimulus of personal interests, the awakening of curiosity and emotion. Kinds of activity which are selective rather than universal need to be encouraged. The most obvious is reading and it is fairly satisfactory that reading is still almost holding its own against less selective activities such as " viewing " and " listening ".

Yet even with the best conceivable early education there will be many—perhaps an appreciable number in the whole population—who will find the reading of books, even novels, uncongenial or unwelcome. For these it seems that what their schooling should do is to show the pleasure to be obtained from hobbies—from carpentry, gardening and many others—and also from the arts. It seems paradoxical that creative work in fabrics, clay and wood is often far more active in primitive societies than it is in our own. Much more than at present could be done towards making known these techniques and towards stimulating the enjoyment of their results, as expressed in colour and design. Equally promising is the possibility of building up a real practising interest in music and drama; that is to say not merely enjoyment as it comes to the onlooker but the actual playing of instruments, and singing and play-acting in choral and drama societies.

If such aims for education, over and above existing ones, may seem excessive it needs to be remembered that there are, or will be, other places for achieving them as well as the schools. In the latter learning of the traditional kind must continue to have pride of place; but there are also the adult education centres and eventually, it may be hoped, there will be the county colleges. From these a great deal is to be expected.

Externality and Inwardness

Towards the counteracting of nihilism, which has been the subject of this chapter, an important quality of mind is inwardness. "Almost all the world," remarked Ortega y Gasset, " is in tumult, is beside itself, and when man is beside himself he loses his most essential attribute: the possibility of meditating, or withdrawing into himself in order to come to terms with himself and define what it is that he believes, what he truly esteems and what he truly detests."[4]

Before saying more about this kind of periodic looking inwards, so clearly described in the passage, it seems useful to mention the converse quality—which may be called externality—and also the quality of objectiveness.

By externality I mean the cast of mind which is almost continuously outgoing and busy with affairs, tending to see far greater reality in what is taking place in the external world of the senses than in the internal world of thoughts, motives and desires. Being thus a quality of alertness far more than of reflectiveness it is distinct from true objectivity. This latter carries with it an understanding of the emotional side of life, for, as John Macmurray has said,[5] there is an objectivity of the emotions as well as of the intellect; emotions are rational and objective when they correspond to the reality of the situation as it actually exists and to achieve this kind of rationality is an important part of a person's development.

Science, which encourges objectiveness, encourages also externality of outlook—and for one reason no doubt because it takes its starting point from the visible and the inanimate. From the viewpoint of the physical sciences man's internal life takes on a character which is secondary and unreal. Science directs our attention towards the world considered much more as an aggregate of things than as a theatre of personal activity, of volition and moral purpose.

Yet it is production and commerce, far more than science, which tend towards the prevailing externality of outlook. The kind of man whom the commercial system holds up for admiration is not the reflective person but rather he who is often loosely called the "extrovert"; the man whose inner life is less active than his interest in material things and affairs; the man who must be doing something, acquiring something.

This preoccupation with the external and physical is actually very far from assisting that objectivity of the emotions of which Macmurray has written. There are many who can talk well about science, or about cars, radio, etc., who are very poor at trying to explain their own feelings or desires. It may be that the result of a concentration of attention on "things" is a failure in the kind of language, the choice of words, which make for a clear expression and analysis of the emotions. And indeed in a scientific world there are signs that parts of this language are falling into disuse. Certain words—"spirit" is an example—have become almost embarrassing because they are so contrary in outlook.

As if by a process of compensation, some of the greatest of modern novelists—Lawrence, Proust, Joyce, Kafka—have been intensely concerned with the subjective. So also has been the philosophy deriving from Kierkegaard. Yet these

movements go sharp against the grain of the prevailing outlook—here what matters is the outward directed personality,
the personality working on the tangible world of nature and
using it as the source of intellectual adventure and power and
plenty. And closely related to this outlook is a strong inclination towards the factual and the literal. In so far as science
helps to set the general tone it sets it in the direction of
ascertainable facts rather than of anything seeming high-
flown or imaginative. The technical society is matter-of-fact,
or nothing.

The converse quality of inwardness is that which has been
described in the passage from Ortega y Gasset—that is to say
it is the ability periodically to retire into oneself, to find one's
bearings and take stock. For this one must be able to exist not
only in a social sense, as a functionary or as a member of a
family, but also sometimes entirely privately. The possibility
of reflection depends on being able to be, for at least part of
the time, on one's own. " Solitude," remarked Thomas Mann,
" gives birth to the original in us. . . ."

As everything becomes more socialized solitude becomes
much harder to come by. People are so busy keeping up an
appearance either of hard work or of sociability that they find
it increasingly difficult to find the periods of privacy when
ideas can be consolidated and emotion straightened out.
Under modern conditions the notion of " meditation " takes
on a meaning which is almost outlandish. How indeed could
one meditate? On the contrary, what the socialized existence
expects of a person, at work or at leisure, is a constant state of
outward receptiveness—that receptiveness which Riesmann
has called " other direction ". Thus in the United States one
of the most valued of professional qualities is an almost un-
varying bonhomie and conviviality. Admirable in its way, it
is the epitome of the " rational " society as described so
slightingly by Kierkegaard. But when, he might ask, in such
an environment is a man able to be truly himself?

In a certain sense reflection is a luxury—which is merely to say that it is not the most necessary of qualities at the level of survival. Yet our society is no longer primitive and it might be thought that one of the benefits of an advanced economy would be a genuine sense of ease. Far from it, alas; it is where the economy is most advanced that the state of being busy, at least among those whom the economy finds most useful, is most intense. The inner attitude—and the world conditions also—which would make this sense of ease a reality have still to be attained. " Time is money," said Benjamin Franklin, and that has been the outlook of industrialism ever since.

Josef Pieper has commented in a similar vein on the loss of the understanding of leisure—and by leisure he means not idleness or amusement but the contemplative life. " The original conception of leisure, as it arose in the civilized world of Greece, has, however, become unrecognizable in the world of planned diligence and ' total labour '; and in order to gain a clear notion of leisure we must begin by setting aside the prejudice—our prejudice—that comes from over-valuing the sphere of work."[6]

Work as overvalued! This represents an attitude of mind in complete contrast to that which prevails in industrial society. We find ourselves more readily in agreement with Simone Weil who believed that our modern vocation is to found a civilization based on the spiritual nature of work. " The thoughts relating to a presentiment of this vocation . . . are the only original thoughts of our time, the only ones we have not borrowed from the Greeks."[7] Yet these two points of view are not entirely opposed; what Pieper argues so well in his essay is that, over against the concept of work (which of course he agrees is essential) and of knowledge which is based on work, there is also a kind of knowledge which is contemplative and receptive. It is this which he believes is denied in industrial society with its overvaluation of work. In this society the scholar himself undergoes a metamorphosis and must call himself an intellectual worker: "he, too, is harnessed to the social system and takes his place in the division of labour; he is allotted his place and his function among the workers; he is a functionary in the world of 'total work '; he may be called a specialist, but he is a functionary."

And thus briefly to summarize: with the coming of industrialism there has been a gradual change from a highly structured and aristocratic kind of society to one which is democratic and " open ", and has the great merit of a strongly developed social conscience. Yet this society is also one which is " mass ": it has the defects which arise from its uncertain and shifting values, its confusion and incoherence, its sheer largeness of scale. Whether or not our civilization will be able to progress beyond the mass stage, whilst retaining the openness of its democratic system, is difficult to foresee. Much may depend on how automation develops and on whether or not it leads to a re-deployment of human effort on the more individual kinds of work. Much may also depend on whether or not education is able to teach greater self-reliance and independence of mind—and also to show a person that he must occasionally withdraw into himself " in order to come to terms with himself and define what it is that he believes, what he truly esteems. . . ."

CHAPTER VII

SCIENCE AND WORLD CONDITIONS

Science and Competition

IT is very encouraging to the scientist that, in spite of every-thing that has happened, the general state of feeling towards science is still as favourable as it is; evidently the majority of people feel that the vast gains which have been made have been worth the immense risks. Even so, the last two decades have brought home, as never before, the equivocal character of scientific advance. Almost every new scientific achievement must be greeted warily, while the competitive world situation continues, as if it were a potential hazard.

Among scientists these decades have seen a loss of innocence and a loss of certainty. The knowledge that science has become deeply involved with the power principle has been one of the facts of life since Hiroshima. And scientists have become aware also of a certain compulsiveness in how they go about their work. This was perhaps best expressed by Oppenheimer in his evidence on the development of the H-bomb: " . . . it is my judgement in these things that when you see something that is technically sweet you go ahead and do it. . . ."[1] Against the force of this attraction, wherever it may lead, the scientist has to be on his guard. It is almost too easy for him to do research and to say of its results " This is none of my business."

Science has become, in a sense, the prisoner of its own success. Certain technical developments grow like snowballs —and not because they are certainly beneficial but rather because they seem dictated by the irrational pressure of events. The most obvious example is weapons development. Although research results are never predictable in advance, the probability that *some* invention or discovery will be made depends on the amount of effort and is greatly affected by the scale of organization and the outlay of money. Thus each nation's security comes to rely on an almost continuous increase of expenditure. Defence research develops like a tropical growth and effloresces in directions we might otherwise regard as fantastic: hydrogen bombs, bacterial warfare, nerve gas, intercontinental missiles. One such invention gives rise to another and the end of the process is not foreseeable. The logic of the situation is that one must develop all weapons *that can be thought of*; for if they can be thought of they may already have been developed by the opposing side.

To be sure this kind of situation is to be expected where defence is concerned. Yet the same kind of compulsiveness, arising from the process of circular causation in a highly competitive environment, is to be found in several other branches of applied science. Has the invention of flight been of value or not on balance? The significance of the question lies not in the answer but rather in the very fact that the question itself is seen to be useless; any discussion would be utterly futile and divorced from reality. Once the aeroplane had been invented there was no stopping it; a chain reaction had set in: supersonic aircraft, rockets, intercontinental missiles; the whole process was outside rational control.

The same may be said of automation. As yet there is no really firm consensus of opinion about whether the long-term effects of automation will prove beneficial or not in total; in my view they probably will. Yet any consideration of its merits and demerits seems entirely academic. At conferences of engineers on this subject one does not find them discussing whether or not automation is socially useful; there is rather the feeling that they are faced with something that is *bound to happen*. The only thing they are left with is to go ahead with the greatest speed, achieving what is inevitable as rapidly as possible. In this, as in many other branches of technology, there is a certain fatalism, an almost Spenglerian sense of necessity.

This all means that there has been a big change in the moral basis of applied science. One can no longer think with honesty that applied science is carried out *because* of social improvement; the latter is almost incidental and, when we speak of the urgent need for more science and technology, however much we may have hopes of genuine benefit, it is always the brute facts of the power situation which is the basis of our real meaning. To be sure there is an awareness that many people are still living in very poor conditions and there is an awareness also of the immensely greater poverty of the underdeveloped areas. Yet it would be unrealistic not to admit that neither of these factors have much bearing on the driving force of applied science in the industrialized countries. They are not the factors having the largest influence either on national research expenditure or on the personal incentives of individual scientists.

During recent years the whole atmosphere of technology has thus become far more elemental than it was. Being no longer associated with the spirit of reform within a society which is essentially secure, the moral force which applied science retains is quite simply patriotic—it is the belief in one's country holding its own. An earlier assumption that science is almost automatically pacific and humanitarian now seems ingenuous. Science is no longer well-being so much as power. In a world whose political institutions have not yet adapted themselves to the changes in man's real circumstances, the best that scientists can do is to work for a better understanding of science's consequences in all of their complexity and to use personal judgement concerning the research projects they feel it right to take up.

Science as a Stabilizing Force

Although in one sense science and technology have thus become subordinated to competition, it needs also to be said that in another sense they work against it. Science, pure and applied, offers its own particular ways and means towards world stability, if these could be seized.

One of them is internationalism of outlook—an attitude of mind which comes far more naturally to the scientist or scholar than it does to the politician. The latter thinks mainly in terms of party or country. But when we discuss biology or medicine, engineering, archaeology or ancient history, the meaning is everywhere the same, the significance is world-wide.

One of the useful forces tending towards stability is therefore the international free-masonry of scholarship which it may be hoped that governments will continue to do everything to encourage. As well as the periodic conferences, where scholars exchange the results of their work, there are also certain organizations achieving collaboration in a more continuous form. Such for example are the International Unions of Astronomy and Chemistry, of Geodesy and Geophysics. These were formed as early as 1919 and were followed by several other unions of special sciences, together with a coordinating body, the International Council of Scientific Unions. No doubt the best known of its many achievements has been the organization of the Geophysical Year.[2]

Similar in spirit to the scientific unions but having a much stronger stabilizing influence are the various international agencies. Many of these are scientific or technical in character and they include the Food and Agriculture Organization, U.N.E.S.C.O., the World Health Organization, the International Labour Office and several others.

Many have felt disappointed with the United Nations, forgetting the very important achievements of the agencies;

for example, the work of F.A.O. in locust control and in preventing the spread of plant pests and diseases from one country to another; the various international fellowships and exchange schemes administered by U.N.E.S.C.O.; the achievements of the World Health Organization in the elimination of malaria, tuberculosis and other diseases; and the work of the same body in the setting up of the Epidemic Intelligence Service whose broadcasts are received daily by health authorities, ships and ports. Less striking but almost equally valuable work is being done by the agencies concerned with safety in civil aviation, with postal services and the allocation of wavelengths, and with meteorology.

This, it may be, is the shape of things to come—the development of organizations which are international in scope and quite distinct from the national states. In the agencies there is already the nucleus of an international civil service having a certain new conception of obligation and loyalty. And although the directorates of the agencies do not, at present, have much real power—not at least by comparison with the national governments—this may not always be the case. A suggestive analogy is the evolution of industrial companies; here the effective power, though it is still legally vested in the shareholders, has passed firmly into the hands of the salaried managers. A similar change may give rise to a slow growth in the strength of the agencies relative to the national governments. That international bodies can become factors to be reckoned with has been shown repeatedly in post-war history.

In short, if peace can be achieved for a few more decades, the agencies may gain sufficient strength to act as a matrix holding together the national states. Apart from its H-bombs and its rockets, the world has certain very difficult problems— scarce raw materials, the food supply, the " population explosion "—which can best be solved internationally. If we could properly take hold of these problems, using them to transcend national self-interest, the competitive forces would retreat into the background.

No doubt the growth of technocracy is not without its dangers and some remarks concerning these will be made later. Yet it is important that we should make use of the creative force of technology and management wherever it is of value. Collaboration at the practical level is a new and promising means of stabilization which is peculiar to our period and is congenial to its technical outlook. By building up on this basis the power politics of the national states might eventually be sidetracked.

Needs for Science apart from Competition

If the cold war and all forms of international tension were magically to cease, what further need would there be for pure or applied science? This question, though it is so hypothetical, should be asked in all seriousness; it can help to show if there are social benefits to be obtained from science which are genuine—genuine in the sense of being required over and above the exigencies of competition—and thereby in which directions science might serve us most usefully.

The answer, it could be argued, is that there would be no further need; our existing techniques, if they were adequately used and disseminated, would be sufficient to provide everyone with a good enough living standard. What is called the urgency for more science, according to this view, arises only from competition. There is little point in going beyond the highest living standards already attained; these high standards, as they exist in the U.S. and in Sweden, give rise to a kind of alienation and nothing has yet emerged to fill the vacuum caused by easy living and short hours.

That kind of argument seems unacceptable. While it can reasonably be said that at present there is probably less real need for further scientific advance than there was earlier, when less had been attained, it should also be said that, under the entirely peaceable conditions envisaged, we could begin to make immeasurably better use of science than previously.

There are probably few who would deny the value of further advances in medicine; and especially perhaps in the field of mental ill-health, where research has been much retarded through lack of funds. Large numbers of people are handicapped, and perhaps unnecessarily so, because of mental weaknesses which are curable. The great problem of cancer remains unsolved and this is a disease which carries away large numbers in their best years. And again only a little progress has so far been made with the disabling diseases of the tropics, the causes of immense misery and suffering.

Science may be needed also to help solve the problem of population—a problem more menacing in some respects than the bomb. No doubt The Pill is on its way; yet there will be many who will be unwilling to use it, or unable. The alternative is an immense expansion of the food supply—and this is desperately needed for present numbers alone. This may require the development of quite novel forms of food; from the sea, or by synthesis from the carbon dioxide in the air, or by the growing of algae in vast ponds to be constructed in the deserts.

Obviously desirable though they are, these prospective advances in medicine and in the means of sustenance should not be thought of as if they could be obtained without corresponding advances in quite different fields. The general experience of science is entirely to the contrary. Advances in medicine may well be determined by achievements over a broad front in all branches of biology, and these achievements in their turn may have to await increased knowledge in chemistry and physics. The advance of one branch of science is assisted by another—and is also assisted by the progress of engineering and all branches of technology. For example, the availability of new drugs is dependent on the chemical industry and the improvement of X-ray equipment and accelerators for hospitals is determined by electrical engineering.

Apart from what has been said about medicine and food supplies, there are other prospective developments in applied science which could greatly improve the conditions of living. One of these would be a miniature battery driven car. Sooner or later the petrol and diesel engines must surely be banished from the streets. Also it seems likely that vehicles for town use will have to be made very much smaller than at present; the area of road surface within the cities is not sufficient to allow a full-sized car to every citizen. With the prospect of off-peak electricity becoming cheaper, the use of batteries (or possibly fuel cells) to drive the citizen's bubble car would become extremely attractive—and incidentally would result in a great reduction in noise and fume.

Putting the matter more generally, the continuance of applied science is to be justified less by what industrial society is now than by what it could be in its next phase. Some of the possible objectives have been mentioned in earlier chapters—and all of them are dependent on a flourishing condition of the economy and this in its turn on the expansion of the industrial system and the furtherance of applied science.

And, of course, science is of value for something else as well as its applications. The joy of science, as it is to the scientist, is not readily accessible to others, for lack of the particular form of specialist training. But for all that, the results and methods of science are gradually assimilated: physics and geology have led to a better understanding of man's place in the universe; psychology has given rise to a much more tolerant attitude towards the variations of behaviour; and science as a whole has had an important influence as a methodology—i.e. as showing how to investigate by use of hypothesis and experiment. And closely related to this is the universality of science—its demonstration of a certain ideal of how one person or one nation can achieve understanding with another through a joint respect for the truth.

In short I have been arguing that there would continue to be an ample future for pure and applied science if the competitive situation did not exist. Yet if such circumstances were ever to arise it would probably become desirable to make a new assessment of the most useful directions for scientific effort. A large part of the available research funds would surely be diverted away from physics and related fields (now obtaining the lion's share on account of defence and prestige) towards biology and the social sciences.

What can be expected from £10,000,000 spent on pure or applied physics? A single large telescope giving some extra knowledge of the universe, or a nuclear machine which might carry forward a little the project for obtaining energy from the thermo-nuclear reaction. Yet this is not a large sum as things go in such work and the cost of putting rockets up to the moon is immensely larger. Some good may come of exploring the solar system—no one can say. Certain it is that there are no planets which can be reached which offer conditions suitable for human life for any prolonged period. This fact has to be weighed against the cost of what would be a superb adventure.

What might be expected from £10,000,000 spent on the biological or social sciences? Such is a princely sum compared with what is given at present for the study of cancer or the tropical diseases, for research on mental illness and many other of humanity's ailments, or for the more fundamental biological research on which medical advances may depend. It is much more than princely compared with what is now available for research on population control, or for the study of the workings of the mind or of human society. As remarked already, psychology has done much to raise the tolerance shown by one person for another. If really worthwhile sums were now given for a worldwide study of the psycho-pathology

7

of nations, might this not do a great deal to increase tolerance between the states and to improve international relations?

By thinking in terms of such comparisons one surely comes to the conclusion that the competitive world situation gives rise to a serious imbalance in research expenditure. Any relaxation of tension which has the prospect of continuing should be made the occasion for an important overhaul of priorities.

The Control of Research Expenditure

What part should scientists play in an overhaul of this kind —or indeed in determining the total spending on science under existing conditions? Almost everyone will agree that there is the need for government to have close contacts with science, and also for the electorate as a whole to be adequately informed and to have scientific understanding. It is a different question how far scientists should have control over the total expenditure of public money on research, or over its broad division between the physical, biological and social sciences.

Every scientist is aware of the self-generating enthusiasm which accompanies rapid progress. In some particular field new ideas and new discoveries suddenly come forward like an avalanche and often with very little bearing on what society most needs at the time. Rocketry is one example; its rapid advance has become an international nuisance. Scientists working in such a field—or in the related branches of " pure " science—find it almost impossible to stand aside. On the contrary the prevailing emotion, overcoming all hesitation, is one of intense interest and excitement. What this means is that certain problems—for example the discovery of new kinds of fuel or the understanding of the rates of chemical reactions at very high temperatures—take on an apparent urgency and significance that no one felt them to have previously. New scientific conferences are arranged, journals are founded, institutes and research centres are established.

There is also the realization, to put the matter frankly, that scientific reputations can be made and that the opportunity offers itself for the building up of powerful research empires. In short there is a general atmosphere of expansion and with it an urgent demand for funds for the particular field. No one in other branches of science will be willing to object; in so far as a " break-through " has taken place, it is part of their overall loyalty to science to wish for this break-through to be supported by whatever sums of money it may require.

What has just been said applies as strongly in pure science as in applied. Indeed there is very little science which can properly be called " pure " when seen from the viewpoint of public support. What may seem the purest of pure science studies is immensely affected—in regard to the pace of its development, the number of workers engaged and the ease of achieving recognition—by the expectation of eventual application. This may be seen, for example, in the expansion of nuclear and theoretical physics. To many of the scientists involved the latter at least may seem a " pure " study. Yet the possibility of supporting their work from public funds is determined by what society expects to gain.

Science to the scientist is clearly a vested interest. This means that whenever it is a question of deciding on the overall priority of science (as compared to expenditure on roads, education, etc.), or of determining the division of funds between different large groups of sciences, the presence of more than a minority of top-ranking scientists in government could be an important factor working against the interests of the public. The belief in science, and also personal loyalties, would be too much involved. Also their non-scientific colleagues in government might often feel impelled to defer to them when in fact they should not.

At the same time it must be accepted that modern governments can defend their countries' economic and military interests only if they are thoroughly well informed in science.

For this purpose many leading scientists and engineers need to be used as *advisers*. To keep them as advisers—and not as policy makers—it is essential that parliament and government should contain a large proportion of men and women whose intellectual training has been over a sufficiently broad front—a training which has given them a genuine understanding of science without creating in them any special loyalties. In this, as in other respects, much might be gained if general degree courses containing both science and non-science subjects were more widely studied. P.P.E. at Oxford has been an important influence but contains no science. Let us suggest physics, economics and history as one of several alternative combinations which would include a science subject to a fairly advanced level.

Technocracy

The point which has been discussed—the control of science's total expenditure—is clearly one aspect of the far more general question of " technocracy "—that is to say of the tendency, within the most industrialized countries, for the technical specialists and high level administrators to gain steadily in power relative to the professional politicians. Since the appearance of Burnham's well-known book *The Managerial Revolution* in 1941 the signficance of the technocratic movement has been taken far more seriously in the U.S. and on the Continent than it has in Britain. Yet the emergence of various international agencies and functional bodies, such as the Coal and Steel Community, is an impressive enough demonstration of what those who have been called " technocrats " have been able to achieve.

It was suggested earlier that technical collaboration, as it manifests itself in the work of these various international organizations, can be a very valuable stabilizing influence. So much to the good. Yet Meynaud[3] and other critics of the movement are surely entirely right when they see in the rise of technocracy a serious danger to the continuance of democratic self-government. What is in question here is the exercise of authority and responsibility within the various countries. Under industrial conditions it is not only the details of administration but also the important policy decisions at cabinet level which require the constant use by governments of scientists, engineers, economists and many others having various forms of expert knowledge. The resultant transfer of a good deal of real power from the elected politician to the expert represents a significant loss of control by the electorate.*

It is not, of course, that there has taken place—or is likely to take place—any change in the formal structure of government. The Cabinet is formed by the party which has been elected. The danger lies rather in the possibility that the democratic structure will become a façade—one which will be piously preserved but will no longer correspond to the reality. Technocracy could become the system, as Meynaud puts it, " permettant de vider progressivement la démocratie d'une partie de son contenu ".

Some part of the solution to this problem will surely be on the lines discussed in the previous section: that is to say, the development of a style of general education which goes some way to enable the non-specialist to meet the challenge of the specialist—or at least of that particular kind of specialist whose potential power is greatest. This is undoubtedly the scientist.

The arguments for putting more science into general education—for achieving " numeracy " as well as literacy— have sometimes been wrongly understood and especially from the side of the humanities. Surely the essential reason is not the facilitation of economic advance (though, of course, this is immensely important); it is rather the desirability that everyone within a democracy should have a clear intellectual

* Cf. the immense authority gained by Lord Cherwell during the war.

grasp of the scientific and technical forces which are determining his future; and further that all who are given power
by the electorate—whether in local or in national government
—should have sufficient technical knowledge to be able, in
the first place, to choose the right specialists for expert advice,
and secondly to keep these experts from gaining control.

In Britain the " humanities "—as they are represented in
schools and universities—have been exceedingly stiff-necked.
They have had almost nothing to do with science or technology. If one believes, as surely one must, that the humanities—when these are conceived in a comprehensive sense—
are of more enduring value than the sciences, and also that
they form the most essential part of the education of the
politician, administrator and civil servant, it is of the greatest
importance that an education in the humanities should be
accompanied by studies in science. Those who are trained
only in the humanities will have progressively less and less
grasp of the world as it is. Their influence will diminish—as
indeed it has been diminishing already for some time.

Towards a Shift of Interest

In the West over a period of a few centuries there has been
an immense change in men's interests. Many of the most
active and fertile minds went into theology during the Middle
Ages, but now go into industry or science. The chief monu-
ments that earlier period left behind were churches and
cathedrals; what we shall now give to posterity are power
stations, dams, bridges, and vast office buildings like the
Empire State. Production, as theology was earlier, has
become the overriding concern.

There have been other societies and civilizations which
likewise concentrated a large part of their attention on some
particular interest. Some put all their best energies into
ritual or the arts, others into war and conquest. Yet there were
still others which seem in retrospect to have achieved a much

more equally balanced state of development—one which was capable of satisfying the spirit of man simultaneously in many different directions.

Surely our own civilization should aim at achieving a similar state of balance. And this for reasons of civilization's safety and continuance, as well as for the better satisfaction of individual men.

No doubt competition, in one form or another, has existed always. Yet the essence of our present situation is that man's competitive instincts have gained greatly in their opportunities to exert themselves and have been provided with weapons of an unparalleled destructiveness. The counteracting impulses, which undoubtedly exist, have not found encouragement to the same extent. Everywhere in our power-ridden world we must aim at changing the balance in favour of the aptitudes and inclinations which are least concerned with power. In this matter those who are teachers can obviously have great influence. In all countries the aim must be to guide the new generation into taking charge of the immense forces now at human disposal with safety and compassion. This must surely mean the fostering of an attitude of mind which is no longer that of an excessive dynamism and possessiveness; rather one which includes a sense of proportion and serenity. The attainment of a major shift in men's interests seems likely to be the only path along which, in the long term, our civilization is likely to survive. And also, in a far more constructive sense, there is still an immense amount that science and industry can do that is worthwhile if the scientific and industrial system can be brought into harmony with the other side of men's natures.

Science, Industry and Society

A more active social criticism of science and industry could also be an important influence. We are in need of the kind of intellectual system which would help to bring the power motives, as they affect the using of science, under a greater degree of rational control. A suggestive analogy is the body of church doctrine which, during the Middle Ages, imposed a degree of order and sanction on the otherwise prevailing rapacity of the period. Theology is a critical and evaluative activity, as are also aesthetics and literary criticism. Yet industry and applied science, although they play an ever increasing part in men's lives, have grown up without the appearance of any corresponding critique.[4]

It might be argued that such a critique already exists—that it is the science of economics. Yet this is not really the case, for economics is not concerned with the value judgements on which decisions have to be based. What are the relative amounts the country should spend on welfare, education, defence, etc.? How highly do we rate clean air as against the cost of installing smoke prevention devices? The answering of almost all such questions depends on considering the social requirements in relation to the available resources, and the value judgements are the ultimate arbiters.

A social criticism would mean also an exploration of the nexus of ideas connecting technology with the main fabric of civilized thought—with the arts, with social history and with politics and economics. During the 19th century the links were allowed to weaken and industrial life became sadly cut off from the arts and from literature. With the appearance of Coketown, industry became a thing apart and technology was given associations of ideas which only now it is beginning to live down.

Technology is thus deficient in its connections with other activities and in this respect compares unfavourably with medicine. The latter is the one branch of applied science which has been well integrated in Western culture,[5] resulting in a high degree of responsibility in the manner of its use. Other branches do not have any ethical criterion concerning how science should be used which is at all comparable with the Hippocratic oath.

Much might be gained if technologists would become more political in their outlook—not necessarily in the party sense, but rather in having a continual awareness of what science is doing to society and clear ideas on what is truly useful and what is not. Technologists—although with many exceptions —usually accept the existing state of affairs somewhat un-critically[6] and in applied science circles generally there is not often a very live political interest. Or rather, to put the matter more accurately, there is not the interest in the *social* condition as distinct from the *economic* condition. The assumption is rather that the two are the same.

The rectifying of this state of affairs could be one of the useful aims of higher technological education. In several of the colleges and universities what are called General or Liberal Studies are gaining ground and this is very much to be welcomed.

Another important matter is the great technical influence of the United States—and the growing influence of Russia. This tends too readily to the view that other countries must necessarily follow the United States or Russia in regard to the kind of society they must evolve. Yet, as was remarked earlier, these are very special countries having immense natural resources and low densities of population. The necessity for Britain and Western Europe and for Asia may be for something different.

And not the necessity only but also the choice. Britain, Europe and the countries of Asia have their own particular traditions of civilization extending back over millenia. With all this richness of the past still in existence, pervading almost every aspect of European and Asian living, the direction to be taken by European and Asian societies, though using science and industry to the best advantage, will surely be neither wholly American nor wholly Russian.

In conclusion, can one define a distinctively European outlook on applied science, an outlook linking up with earlier traditions? In Renaissance times there was a spirit of immense zest and enthusiasm in technology, and such a close liaison between the useful and the fine arts that it might be hard to say where the one merged into the other. By the 19th century much of this sense of unity had been lost and there had developed a separation between the " pure " and the " applied " in science, and between industry and the arts. At present there are useful movements towards healing these gaps and towards forming an outlook on applied science which would see it more closely in relation to society. Linked with this has been the growth of the social conscience and the realization that the improvements in living conditions obtainable through science must be given out on an equitable basis.

Yet there are many potential improvements apart from the more plentiful supply of goods. Many might like to see more beauty and serenity in the urban environment, more enjoyment obtainable from the working day, more opportunities in leisure through better education. Thus a consistent attitude towards the purposes of technology may be expressed in terms of a modern conception of social justice and economic advancement, together with a much earlier European idea of the " good life " and the unity of the arts and sciences.

And indeed technology is a bridge between science and the humanities, being science in human use. Yet here we have to tread rather warily for the world of techniques should be kept in its proper place. Though we obtain great value from science, we should avoid what is often associated with the technical outlook—a tendency towards an excess of organization and planning. People need to keep for themselves the opportunities to do as they like.

NOTES AND REFERENCES

Chapter I

1. GUNNAR MYRDAL, *Beyond the Welfare State*, p. 112, Duckworth, London 1960.
2. C. P. SNOW, *Science and Government*, Oxford 1961.
3. ALEXANDER FLECK, *Science and Industry*, The Fawley Foundation Lecture 1960, Southampton University.

Chapter II

1. J. L. & B. HAMMOND, *The Rise of Modern Industry*, p. 217, Methuen 1926.
2. J. M. KEYNES, *The End of Laissez-Faire*, The Hogarth Press, London 1926.
3. K. GALBRAITH, *The Affluent Society*, Hamish Hamilton, London 1958.
4. This was actually the case in canon law more than in civil. See for example W. J. ASHLEY, *English Economic History and Theory*, Vol. I.
5. JEAN GIMPEL, *Les Bâtisseurs de Cathédrales*, Editions du Seuil, Paris 1958.
6. H. PIRENNE, *Economic and Social History of Medieval Europe*, p. 186, Kegan Paul, London 1936.
7. The evidence concerning the suppression of an improved lathe at Nuremberg in 1578 is given by F. KLEMM, *A History of Western Technology*, p. 153, Allen & Unwin, London 1959.
8. L. SCOTT, *Fillipo di Ser Brunellesco*, London 1901.
9. PAUL FAURE, *La Renaissance*, Presses Universitaires de France, Paris 1949. For some useful remarks on the new attitude to wealth which developed from the 15th century onwards, see D. HAY, *The Italian Renaissance*, p. 126 ff., Cambridge 1961.
10. J. U. NEF, *Cultural Foundations of Industrial Civilization*, Ch. II, Cambridge 1958.
11. For further discussion of this aspect of technology see S. GIEDION, *Mechanisation Takes Command*, Oxford University Press, New York 1948. Giedion believes that the conveying of a sense of the miraculous was generally

regarded at this period as being a more important use of invention than production.

12. In this connection see L. ROBBINS, *The Theory of Economic Policy in English Classical Political Economy*, Macmillan, London 1952.

13. JOSIAH WEDGWOOD (1730-95) might be cited as a counter-example, but had few successors in the same style.

14. RICHARD BAXTER, *A Christian Directory*, Part I, Ch. x, London 1678.

15. This is not necessarily to support the theory that Protestantism had a large influence in forming the outlook of capitalism (whose beginnings had indeed pre-dated the Reformation). It is rather to assert that Protestantism tended towards increasing the productivity of capital.

16. An important discussion on how Puritanism favoured the development of science, through its emphasis on practical activity and " remaking the world ", etc., is given by R. K. MERTON, *Osiris* 1938, Vol. IV, pp. 360-632.

17. For an interesting survey of the influences of the industrial revolution on the graphic arts, see F. D. KLINGENDER, *Art and the Industrial Revolution*, Noel Carrington, London 1947.

18. See especially the address at Bradford in *The Two Paths* (1859) and *Time and Tide by Weare and Tyne* (1867).

19. Concerning Germany see KLEMM (loc. cit., p. 335). He writes erroneously, however, of the phenomenon *not* having occurred in Britain.

20. A. URE, *The Philosophy of Manufactures*, p. 368, 1st Edn., London 1835.

21. H. FORD, *My Life and Work*, p. 19, Heinemann, London 1931.

22. Reasons why a democracy prefers private to public goods—and thus tends to be dilatory in the provision of roads, educational facilities, etc.—have been discussed by L. ROBBINS, *The Economic Problem in Peace and War*, Macmillan, London 1950. See also K. GALBRAITH's well known *The Affluent Society*.

23. On industrialism as contributing towards a Christian state of society see MIDDLETON MURRY, *The Free Society*, Dakers, London 1958.

24. PIGOU, *The Economics of Welfare*, Macmillan, London 1932.

Chapter III

1. D. G. CHRISTOPHERSON, *On Being a Technologist*, S. C. M. Press Ltd. 1959.
2. RICHARD BAXTER, *The Christian Directory*, Part I, Ch. x, London 1678.
3. See, for example, J. A. C. BROWN, *The Social Psychology of Industry*, Penguin Books 1954.
4. L. MUMFORD, *Technics and Civilization*, Routledge 1934.
5. SIMONE WEIL, *La Condition Ouvrière*, Gallimard, Paris.
6. SIMONE WEIL, *The Need for Roots*, Routledge and Kegan Paul 1952.
7. ERICH FROMM, *The Sane Society*, Routledge and Kegan Paul 1956.
8. GEORGES FRIEDMANN, *Ou va le Travail Humain?*, Gallimard, Paris 1950.
9. GEORGES FRIEDMANN, *Industrial Society*, The Free Press, Glencoe, Illinois 1955.
10. See, for example, F. KLEMM, *A History of Western Technology*, p. 29.
11. *The Book of Trades*, London 1804.
12. HENRY FORD, *My Life and Work*, pp. 80, 83 and 87, Heinemann, London 1931.
13. ADAM SMITH, *The Wealth of Nations*, Book v, Ch. I.
14. For a clear and authoritative account of the various aspects of automation (and the meaning of the term) see an article by Lord Halsbury, *Impact*, Vol. VII, 1956, p. 179 (U.N.E.S.C.O., Paris). Also the report, *Automation* (Department of Scientific & Industrial Research, H.M.S.O. 1956) and *Three Case Studies in Automation* (P.E.P. Political and Economic Planning, London 1957).
15. *The Sane Society*, p. 289.
16. *Technics and Civilization*, p. 411-413.
17. *The Need for Roots*, p. 56.
18. Work teams already exist in certain industries; in this connection see some remarks of C. A. R. CROSSLAND, in an article in *Encounter*, February 1959. See also FRIEDMANN's description of the Societé de Travail (distinct from the Communauté de Travail) in *Industrial Society*, The Free Press, Glencoe, Illinois 1955.
19. One of the best known of the work communities is the one known as Boimondau at Valence, established for the

production of watch cases. Its organization is described by FROMM, *The Sane Society*, p. 306, and by G. FRIEDMANN, *Industrial Society*, p. 343.

20. Concerning the character of industry in relation to social disturbances and the origin of movements such as Nazism, see ERIC HOFFER, *The True Believer*, Secker & Warburg 1952.

21. *La Condition Ouvrière*, p. 259.

Chapter IV

1. Quoted by RAYMOND WILLIAMS, *Culture and Society*, p. 23, Chatto & Windus 1958.

2. ASHTON, *An Economic History of England; the 18th Century*, p. 34, Methuen, London 1955. See also MANTOUX, *La Révolution Industrielle au XVIIIe Siècle*, p. 385, Paris 1906.

3. C. DAWSON, *The Dynamics of World History*, Sheed & Ward, London 1957.

4. R. MATTHEW, *The Listener*, August 6th, 1959.

5. *The Times*, Feb. 13th, 1962, from a White Paper.

6. L. ROBBINS, *The Economic Problem in Peace and War*, Macmillan, London 1950.

Chapter V

1. L. MUMFORD, *Art and Technics*, p. 50. Oxford University Press 1952.

2. HERBERT READ, *Art and Industry*, Faber & Faber, London 1944.

3. See, for example, SYLVIA CROWE, *The Landscape of Power*, The Architectural Press, London 1958.

4. J. K. GALBRAITH, *The Liberal Hour*, Ch. III, Hamish Hamilton 1960. Galbraith remarks that in Europe the business man has come more completely to terms with the artist than he has done so far in the U.S. Some of the imbalance in the American economy Galbraith attributes to the importation of well designed goods from Italy, France and Scandinavia on a very large scale.

Chapter VI

1. B. PASTERNAK, *Dr. Zhivago*, Ch. 13, Section 14.

2. W. R. NIBLETT, *Education and The Modern Mind*, p. 91, Faber & Faber 1954.

3. JOHN MACMURRAY, B.B.C. pamphlet, *Learning to Live.*
4. ORTEGA Y GASSET, *Man and People,* Ch. I, Allen & Unwin 1957.
5. JOHN MACMURRAY, *Reason and Emotion.*
6. JOSEPH PIEPER, *Leisure the Basis of Culture,* p. 26, Faber & Faber, 1952.
7. SIMONE WEIL, *The Need for Roots.* Trans. A. F. Wells, Routledge & Kegan Paul.

Chapter VII

1. J. R. OPPENHEIMER. Quoted by R. Jungk, *Brighter Than a Thousand Suns,* p. 266, Penguin Books 1960.
2. For an account of the work of I.C.S.U. by its former Secretary-General, Sir Harold Spencer Jones, see *Endeavour,* April 1959, pp. 88-92.
3. JEAN MEYNAUD, *Technocratie et Politique,* Publ. M. Meynaud, Lausanne 1960. See also JACQUES ELLUL, *La Technique ou l'enjeu du siècle,* Armand Colin, Paris 1954, and JACQUES BILLY, *Les Techniciens et le Pouvoir,* Presses Universitaires, Paris 1960.
4. In a footnote to *Capital* (Everyman Edition, p. 392) Marx deplored the lack in his time of any critical history of technology. Since then there have been published several histories, although not very critical ones, and also discussions on the place of applied science in society such as J. D. BERNAL's important book, *The Social Function of Science* (Routledge 1939).
5. c.f. A. E. CLARK-KENNEDY, *The Art of Medicine in Relation to the Progress of Thought,* Cambridge 1945.
6. On the technologist as a conformist see MAX LERNER's article, " Big Technology and Neutral Technicians ", in *Perspectives,* No. 14, 1956.